ART OF THE DIGITAL AGE

Thames & Hudson

First published in the United Kingdom in 2006 by
Thames & Hudson Ltd, 181A High Holborn, London WC1V 7QX

www.thamesandhudson.com

British Library Cataloguing-in-Publication Data
A catalogue record for this book is available from
the British Library

ISBN-13: 978-0-500-23817-2
ISBN-10: 0-500-23817-0

Designed by SMITH
Victoria Forrest
Printed and bound in China by C & C Offset Printing

JOHN F. SIMON, JR., *ALIFE*, 2003.
SOFTWARE, MACINTOSH POWERBOOK G4,
ACRYLIC PLASTIC, 45.7 X 50.8 X 5.1 CM
(18 X 20 X 2 IN)

CONTENTS

Acknowledgments

I dedicate this book to my sister Alice, whose encouragement and support over the years have nurtured my interest in art. I would like to thank David Rhodes, President of the School of Visual Arts, for his generous support of this project; Deborah Hussey and Maryalice Quinn, whose hard work, help and energy made this book a reality; and Joe Meyer and my graduate assistants Arlene Ducao and Ju Hyun Yoo, for their help with research and with the production of the book. Finally, I'd like to thank sincerely all of the artists who have contributed their work to this endeavour.

PREFACE

My involvement with digital art began in 1976, when I was a graduate student at Syracuse University. I was enrolled in an experimental studio course in which we created drawings by programming the university's mainframe computer. Although computer graphics were still at an embryonic stage, the potential of this new medium was apparent. The computer could draw with far more precision than the human hand, and the mathematical nature of programming offered me new conceptual and creative territory.

Over the past three decades I have seen incredible developments in digital art, and in recent years there has been a growing international interest in the art form. Digital tools have become ubiquitous, and the number of artists using them continues to grow. Several international art centres have supported digital art for many years, and an increasing number of museums and galleries around the world are now exhibiting this work.

The idea for this book grew out of the tenth anniversary celebration of the New York Digital Salon, established in 1993 to host an annual exhibition of digital art in New York and to foster an international awareness of art created with the latest technology. It is my hope that *Art of the Digital Age* will achieve the same aim: that by defining digital art through an overview of its history, its recent advances and many of most prominent practitioners, this book will serve to inspire those who have not yet begun to create in the digital realm.

Bruce Wands

AN OVERVIEW OF DIGITAL ART

Digital technologies have had, and continue to have, a profound effect on contemporary art and culture. Born out of the electronic revolution, the globalization of mass media, and the internet, digital culture holds even more potential for societal change than television and radio once did. Whereas television and radio are broadcast media and provide only one-way communication, the internet offers the opportunity of interacting with others and allows access to a far greater range of information. We are at a time of unprecedented growth and innovation in the world of digital technologies, and the place of digital media in contemporary society and in our daily lives has been firmly established.

Contemporary artists are using the internet as a new art medium and adopting digital tools and techniques as part of their creative process. The computer has enabled artists to create works, and new types of work, never before possible: intricate images that could not be created by hand; sculptures formed in three-dimensional databases rather than in stone or metal; interactive installations that involve internet participation from around the globe; and virtual worlds within which artificial life forms live and die.

As the boundaries of digital art expanded during the mid-1990s, museums began to take a serious interest in its development. Significant exhibitions of digital art have been held in recent years, showing its increasingly widespread acceptance throughout the contemporary art community. In addition, museums and galleries are bringing their collections of traditional art online, making them easily accessible. As a result, the role and presence of art in society is undergoing considerable change and growth. The art experience extends now to homes, cybercafes and any public or private space where there is internet access or a local area network.

**BONNIE MITCHELL,
ELAINIE LILLIOS AND
GREG CORNELIUS,
EXPERIENTIAL EXTREMISM,
2003–04. INTERACTIVE
AUDIOVISUAL INSTALLATION,
6 X 9 M (20 X 30 FT)**

Experiential Extremism is an
immersive interactive installation
that uses time-based visual and
sonic events to control emotional
and physical responses. The
piece consists of three networked
computers that control real-time,
multi-layered sonic and visual
events, all of which are triggered
by electronic sensors. The project
explores the concept of extremism
in today's society.

SHERBAN EPURÉ,
***CONDOTTIERE,* 2003. INKJET**
PRINT, VARIABLE DIMENSIONS
Sherban Epuré uses the term 'meta-phorms' to describe the results of his mathematically based image-generating process. This work, produced using algorithms, is formed by the interaction of colour with a simple geometric shape. One intent of Epuré's imaging is to forge a link between Western technology and Eastern spirituality.

What is digital art?

Fundamental to any explanation of digital art is an understanding of the context in which we view it – the 'art experience' itself. It can be said that great works of art communicate simultaneously on four levels: sensory, emotional, mental and spiritual. It is this synchronicity of body, heart and mind that helps to define our complex reactions to art, as well as to the everyday world.

The power that electronic and digital media have on us is partly explained by the way in which they appeal to our senses. One simple example is our involuntary visual attraction to motion. If we enter a room with two computers, one showing a static image and the other a moving image, our attention will automatically turn towards the movement. Sound, on the other hand, fills the space we are in and works on us in different ways. While vision and hearing are the dominant physical senses where art is concerned, other senses also have a part to play. Touch, in particular, is an important component in experiencing many contemporary artworks. The traditional museum and gallery etiquette of 'Look, don't touch' cannot be applied to interactive art, which requires the participation of the viewer and can be more accurately described as 'Look, please touch.'

The emotional and intellectual aspects of the ways we experience art are essentially a matter of how effectively an artwork can elicit a response from us. If an artwork fails to awaken any curiosity or to engage viewers on an emotional level, they are unlikely to spend any significant time with it. We may also experience a spiritual link with a work of art – a message that is communicated on an inspirational or non-intellectual, non-emotional level. Simply put, the art touches one's soul. When all of these elements combine, the art experience can become a deeply moving one.

Our experience of viewing art is further influenced by the venue. In the past, where an artwork was exhibited was often a means by which it was classified. If it was in a museum or gallery, it was considered 'art'. There is much to be said for this perspective, since curators are recognized experts in their fields and have an informed knowledge of the pieces they select for exhibition. The art historian also has a vital role, since critical writings associated with a particular artwork or artist help to create credibility.

It should be remembered that making art is far removed from the viewers' experience of it. Artists tend to be more involved with the process than with the end result, and approach the creation of an artwork as both experimental and evolutionary – something especially true of digital artists. Having chosen to use a computer to visualize a work, however, many go on to create the piece using traditional media. The forms that digital art can take – both traditional and new – can be blended in many ways, which sometimes makes the distinctions between them unclear. Traditional forms of digital art include prints, photography, sculpture, installations, video, film, animation, music and performance. New forms that are unique to the digital realm include virtual reality, software art and net art. A more complete understanding of digital art will emerge as we examine its relationship to technology and contemporary art, the way in which these artworks are created, and the inner make-up of the digital artist.

Art and technology

Digital art is intimately linked to science and technology, which are fundamental to its creation and physical substance. Arguments of technological determinism in art proclaim that it is the development of technology that has allowed artists to create these works. However, if we look at art as a creative reflection of modern culture, then digital art can be considered a subset of contemporary art. Since the adjective 'digital' is often ambiguous, and does not clearly define the work's final form, it is here applied to artworks in which artists have used the computer as a primary tool, medium and/or creative partner.

Many curators and critics see digital art as an evolutionary development of the mechanical and electrical processes of photography, film and video. This approach forms part of a larger historical perspective, in which photography itself evolved from drawing and painting. Although initially there was considerable resistance to the concept of photography as fine art, it is now widely recognized as such and occupies a place in the collections of major museums worldwide. Film is a logical evolutionary step from photography: the physical nature of the medium is identical, although differently formatted in order to move through the camera quickly and to capture motion. Video, too, can be thought of as usurping film technology. Likewise, the internet is often considered a development of mass media, best exemplified by radio and television. One interesting aspect of mass media is its ever-increasing inclusivity: while films can contain photographs and video can contain film content and photographs, the internet is capable of communicating through text, image, sound and such time-based media as video and animation. Although an evolutionary approach to digital art based on advances in technology offers only an elementary understanding of how it relates to popular culture, it does provide a historical framework for the development of digital tools and other media now available to contemporary artists.

One dilemma that has arisen with the use of digital technology in art-making is the concept of 'the original'. Paintings are original works of art, traditional printmakers refine a work to end up with an artist proof that sets the standard for an edition of prints, and even photographers have adopted the concept of editions and originals. Since a digital file is stored electronically and can be reproduced with all its elements intact, how does it relate to the concept of the 'original'? Some artists make only a single print from their file and thus have a single original, others make limited editions of their work, and some create open editions. Needless to say, the value of an individual print in the commercial art world is dependent on how many multiples are in circulation, as well as the strength of the market for which it is intended.

A portrait of the digital artist

One way of gaining a better understanding of digital art is to consider the people who create it. Although all are involved in the familiar artistic processes of self-expression and discovery, digital artists can be characterized in several ways: some are also computer programmers who write their own code in order to create the work, whereas others collaborate with programmers and computer technicians in order to realize their creations. Even in these collaborative relationships, artists must have an understanding of both the potential and the limitations of using digital tools, as well as a fairly high level of technical knowledge. Technological curiosity is thus an important facet in the make-up of a digital artist.

Another aspect common to digital artists is a desire to create artworks using new tools and techniques. Although what is 'new' is continuously evolving, many artists were first attracted to digital tools because they offered creative opportunities not possible through traditional means. One benefit that digital tools offer is increased authorial control. This can be both a blessing and a curse, since greater control often means that creative 'accidents' happen less often. On the other hand, deliberately created random effects can provide artists with results they may not have previously considered. For example, an artist may create software that progressively changes an image over time, letting the computer create several hundred variations of an image, then selecting the final images they like best.

JAVIER ROCA, *TOPOGRAPHIC HEAD*, 2002. INKJET PRINT, 99.1 X 32.5 CM (39 X 12.8 IN)
Making full use of the unprecedented level of control that computer software offers over light, shadow and colour, Javier Roca combines traditional figurative illustration with layered elements of the techno-surreal.

JEAN-PIERRE HÉBERT,
UN CERCLE TROP ÉTROIT:
***DÉRIVÉE SECONDE*, 1995.**
INK ON PAPER DRAWING,
48 X 35 CM (18⅞ X 13¾ IN)
Jean-Pierre Hébert is considered
one of the pioneers of digital art.
A self-defined 'algorist', Hébert
uses algorithms as the core of his
software programmes and to drive
his pen plotters. In most of his
works, he incorporates traditional
tools such as pens, pencils,
brushes, magnets and pendulums,
along with exploring alternative
media such as sound and sand.

THOMAS PORETT, *KOI SPACE/TIME*, 1999. IRIS PRINT, 89 X 56 CM (32 X 22 IN)

Although at first glance this may look like a single image, it was in fact constructed from two photographs that were merged using a 2D painting programme. Thomas Porett's work examines tensions between motion and the passage of time.

Digital artists are also risk-takers by nature, and concern for their creative work supersedes any desire to conform to the traditional art establishment. This was especially true in the early days, when digital art was looked upon as outsider art. While there were a few courageous souls experimenting with digital forms in the 1960s, 1970s and 1980s, it is only recently that museums and galleries have begun to take the art form seriously. Although this is a welcome change, it is important to acknowledge those pioneers of digital art who were willing to experiment in unfamiliar territory.

Emerging artists are now growing up with digital literacy as an integrated part of their lives. They will never know a world without the internet, laptop, mobile phones or email, to mention but a few of the technological aids that help to shape our daily existence. As such, these artists do not regard making art with digital tools as anything different from using traditional tools. The qualifier 'digital' has already begun to disappear, and these artists of the future will be considered contemporary artists.

The forms and classification of digital art

Digital art is radically new, and yet many of its facets have grown out of traditional art practice. The current tendency to categorize digital art according to established perspectives will hopefully dissipate enough to allow a deeper understanding of its techniques and purpose to be reached. As digital art continues to take a prominent place in the contemporary art world, and the language and syntax of computer technologies become more refined and familiar, we will be better equipped to define its many forms and cultural contributions.

Digital art most often takes on the form of data – that is, a computer file that exists as a collection of ones and zeros on digital storage media. Sometimes this is the final form, as with net art, in which a physical rendition of the work does not exist. Whether or not this data is transformed into something more concrete depends on the artist. As computers grow more powerful and software more sophisticated, the variety of forms (often referred to as 'polyforms' or 'meta-forms') that the data can assume is increasing. For example, a virtual object created with three-dimensional modelling and animation software can end up as a single image, as animation, or it can be output as sculpture. The animation or image can also be incorporated into a website and thus exist on the internet as net art.

The artworks presented in this book have been categorized primarily according to the final media in which they reside, as well as the intention of each artist and the author's interpretation. The forms of digital art outlined here are based on current state-of-the-art technology and include imaging; sculpture; installation and virtual reality; performance, music and sound art; animation and video; software, database and game art; and net art. In the chapters that follow, these various genres of digital art are explored in greater detail.

Digital imaging

The earliest digital art consisted of printed images drawn with line plotters or dot-matrix printers, or photographs of computer screens. The developments in digital imaging of recent years are due mainly to the rapid growth of digital photography. The popularity of this medium has helped to quicken the development of higher image resolution, so that a continuous tone has been achieved and pixels are no longer visible. It has also facilitated the widespread use of archival pigments and papers, meaning that the life of digital prints has been greatly extended. In addition, a digital file can now be archived safely and easily for future reprints.

Prints can take many forms, from the small-format digital photograph made with archival paper on a desktop printer to specialized prints several feet in height and width. The image can also be integrated with printmaking methods, such as silkscreen; combined with traditional drawing and painting media; or incorporated into installations, sculptures or video displays.

Digital sculpture

The creation of three-dimensional objects using digital technology developed out of computer-assisted design and manufacturing (CAD/CAM). Early machines for producing sculpture digitally consisted of a subtractive process using a milling head, similar to an electric drill or router, which could be controlled in three dimensions. Intricate objects could be created, but artists were limited by the hardware: only the milling head could move, not the medium itself, and only smaller works were possible. New, larger systems are capable of milling both small sculptures and architecturally scaled works with high precision.

The process of rapid prototyping, which developed out of early CAD/CAM technology, is now quite sophisticated. Rather than having a milling head remove material from the art medium, rapid prototyping is an additive process in which extremely thin layers of wax or powder are built up to form a three-dimensional object. Some systems are also capable of

DAN COLLINS, *RETURN TO THE GARDEN*, 2003. NETWORKED VIDEO INSTALLATION WITH SCULPTURAL ELEMENTS

Over the past twenty-five years, Dan Collins has focused on overlapping three areas: digital sculpture, closed-circuit video and anamorphosis. This interactive installation utilized a networked surveillance camera that museum visitors controlled to reveal key aspects of the work. In doing so, Collins asks his audience to reconsider the dialectic between the actual and the virtual by wilfully distorting perspective through video techniques that altered the perception of digital sculptural elements hanging from the ceiling.

JIM CAMPBELL, *PHOTO OF MY MOTHER*, 1996; *PORTRAIT OF MY FATHER*, 1994–95. CUSTOM ELECTRONICS, GLASS, PHOTOGRAPHS, LCD MATERIAL, EACH 121.9 X 30.5 X 30.5 CM (48 X 12 X 12 IN)
Jim Campbell uses his own body tempos to control the rate at which these two images change. In the case of *Photo of My Mother*, he uses an hour-long digital recording of his breath as a timing device: as he exhales, the image changes from clear to foggy, as if breathing onto the glass, and then clears again. For *Portrait of My Father*, he uses a recording of his heartbeat to control the speed at which his father appears and disappears.

using a powder-and-inkjet process that produces objects with millions of colours. Rapid prototyping has advanced to the point that it is easily accessible and affordable. Some artists use the actual prototype as their final form, while others use them as models for a mould from which they then produce a work cast in metal or other media. Sculptors also employ digital laser technologies, which can be used on a wide variety of material. These new processes have revolutionized the way in which physical sculptures can be produced.

Virtual sculpture has emerged as a development of digital sculpture. Here, the sculptural work never assumes the form of an actual physical object but resides as a file within cyberspace or within the virtual world of the computer. Sculptors have previously always been limited by physical forces – gravity, the nature of their materials, the location and size of the sculpture, and so on. In the virtual world, the rules are entirely different. Gravity no longer applies, and size, scale and materials can be changed easily by simply choosing items on a software menu. The artist can examine the work from an infinite number of viewpoints, and he or she can create a virtual, interactive world in which to display it. Understandably, this type of creative control holds great appeal for artists.

Digital installation and virtual reality

Digital technology has greatly increased the range of creative options available to installation artists and it allows them precise control over their work. Early control systems for installation artworks had to be custom-built and were often extremely complex and expensive. Digital technologies such as hardware microcontrollers, sensors and software packages that control machine routines have emerged, allowing for art experiences that were not previously possible. Examples include interactive environments, robotics, and data-driven installations that read real-time information from the internet. This is one of the fastest growing areas of digital art, not only because of the creative control it offers, but also because participatory and interactive art is becoming an important component of contemporary art.

Virtual reality allows for the creation of an immersive experience. That is, the participant or viewer is brought into a completely synthetic world created by the artist. Virtual experiences take different forms depending on the artwork and hardware/software interface that is used: some systems require the viewer to wear a head-mounted display (HMD) or a similar type of interface device, while other virtual experiences are designed for the internet, where three-dimensional worlds can be explored through artificial characters and life-forms. As computing power increases and new interfaces become mass produced, the field of virtual reality appears ready to undergo a renaissance.

Performance, music and sound art

The effects of digital technologies on performance, music and sound art have been mainly evolutionary, but they have also enabled the creation of many new forms of expression. Performance artists have incorporated digital

**TOSHIO IWAI, *PIANO –
AS IMAGE MEDIA*, 1995.
AUDIOVISUAL INSTALLATION**
Here, a virtual score is used to
trigger the keys of a piano,
which in turn induce the projection
of computer-generated images
on a screen. The melodies, as
well as the visuals they produce,
are chosen by gallery visitors.
Toshio Iwai's project establishes
connections between notation,
sound and image, and provides
an almost synaesthetic experience.

technologies into their work in much the same way as installation artists. Technological advances have expanded their creative palette and given them more precise control over their performances. The influence of computers on music and sound art in particular has been nothing short of revolutionary: digital recording software has undeniably made a huge impact, but at the core of the digital music explosion lies the development of the Musical Instrument Digital Interface (MIDI).

Musical Instrument Digital Interface was developed in the mid-1980s, and its original intention was to enable synthesizers from different manufacturers to communicate with each other. MIDI achieved this through storing parameters – such as pitch, note on, note off, duration and tempo – as digital data rather than as an actual sound file. This launched a whole new world for composers. MIDI data can be manipulated like text in a word processor so that harmony parts can be easily added or removed, different instrumental sounds can be heard and changed quickly, sheet music can be generated automatically from a performance (rather than being handwritten), and composers are no longer confined by the physical limitations of a particular instrument. When combined with digital audio recording software, MIDI offers composers and musicians the capabilities of the most sophisticated recording studio on their personal computers; and when converted into a format compatible with MP3 players or the Apple iPod, their work can be distributed via the internet to an international audience.

Digital animation and video
The transition from traditional animation, film and video to their digital counterparts has had profound repercussions both for artists and for the commercial film and broadcast industries. Traditional animation was created entirely by hand; early animators produced literally thousands of

DENNIS H. MILLER, *PAST TENSE 1*, 2001. DIGITAL ANIMATION FRAME
This still frame from *Past Tense* reveals Dennis H. Miller's technique of exploring a defined colour space through background and foreground elements. Dense, morphing textures appear throughout the work and several small referential objects are used to create continuity. Miller's approach to abstract animation also includes the use of highly coloured images that often demonstrate repeating patterns, similar to the use of rhythmic structures in music.

drawings as part of a long and expensive process, which by necessity became a collaborative endeavour. One early influence of computers on animation was the advent of digitally controlled animation cameras, which automated most of the time-consuming camera work. Today, animation makes use of digital production systems whereby drawings are scanned, coloured and composited within the computer before being output to film, video or a digital format such as DVD.

Three-dimensional computer animation is unique to the digital realm and has a completely different look from that of hand-drawn animation. It has been widely adopted by the film and game industries, and a new genre of three-dimensional computer-animated feature films has emerged. In addition, versions of the software used to make these films can now be run on a personal computer, creating new interest among artists working in short-form animation. Dozens of international festivals and a myriad of websites currently offer venues for this type of work.

The production of video has also changed substantially, since artists now have the ability to produce high-quality videos on their personal computers. Technological advances in this area, coupled with the relative affordability of high-quality digital video cameras, have fostered tremendous growth in the independent video movement and have brought video and DVD production into mainstream culture.

BENJAMIN FRY, *VALENCE*, 1999. VISUALIZATION SOFTWARE.

Valence is data-visualization software designed to show structures and relationships between large sets of information. It can be used to analyse anything from literary texts to a series of genomes. Words and discrete pieces of information that are used frequently tend to appear around the screen's outer edges.

Software, database and game art

While most digital media have their roots in traditional art forms, software, database and game art are based solely on the digital. Software and game art can be defined as works of executable code written by an artist, either alone or in collaboration with a computer programmer. The running, or execution, of the programme is what creates the artwork. Examples of software and game art include interactive drawing and music software, algorithmic and generative works, data transformation, net art, artistic games and many others.

Database art is a variation of software art that depends on existing data to form the work's substance. While software art relies on the instructions carried out by a programme, database art concentrates on interpreting an existing body of data for which artists either appropriate databases or create their own. Again, this division is arbitrary and many hybrid forms exist. There are those who feel that this type of digital art is one of the few 'pure' forms of digital art, since it has not evolved directly from traditional media.

Net art

Although artists have been using the internet since its inception, it was during the mid-1990s, when graphical browsers such as Netscape and Internet Explorer were invented, that net art gained prominence. Net art uses the internet as its final medium. It can be thought of as a networked variation of software art, but is separated into its own category because of the large number of artists involved in this type of work. Artists are attracted to the freedom of the internet, the ability to create independent websites without censorship or external controls. This allows them to bypass the traditional gallery and museum establishment and to reach an immediate and international audience. When net art first appeared, it also represented fresh creative territory, with few historical precedents. It has continued to

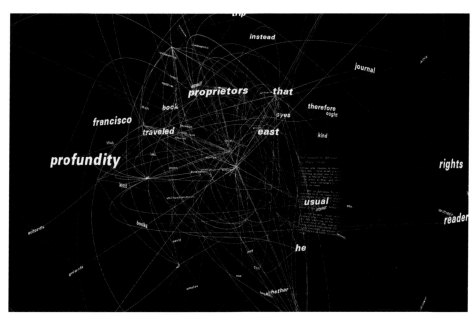

evolve, but has also been a victim of rapid changes in software and hardware: the lifespan of internet hardware and software during the latter part of the 1990s was approximately six months, and upgrades to browser software caused some early work to become obsolete. In spite of these difficulties, the freedom and control artists enjoy in the field of net art have kept it a vibrant art form.

A history of digital art

The roots of digital art are ancient and varied. Indeed, it could be argued that the prehistoric cave-paintings found in France and northern Spain provide not only some of the earliest examples of graphic storytelling, but also the earliest examples of immersive environments. As evidenced by sites such as Stonehenge, by the art and monuments of the Classical antiquity and by the calendar systems of the Mayans, peoples around the world, from the earliest times, considered the disciplines of science, astronomy and mathematics fundamental to their art and culture.

It was during the 19th century, a period in which scientific advances and inventions abounded, that the infrastructure underlying the computer revolution was truly established. In 1834, Charles Babbage conceived of the Analytical Engine, a hand-cranked, mechanical machine for automating calculations that anticipated virtually every aspect of present-day computers. Other events relevant to the history of computing were the invention of the telegraph and Morse code (a primitive precursor of binary code), the design of the first keyboard (initially for the typewriter), and the invention of the telephone by Alexander Graham Bell in 1876. In addition, George Eastman released the Kodak camera and roll film in 1888, which in turn led to the invention of stop-motion animation by George Méliès in 1895. These advances ushered in the era of mechanical and electronic media.

Opposite
BRUCE WANDS, *HEARTLINE*, 1976. PLOTTER DRAWING ON PAPER, 30.5 X 30.5 CM (12 X 12 IN)
This early example of digital image-making was created using the ArtSpeak programming language and printed on a line plotter connected to the IBM 360 mainframe computer at Syracuse University, New York.

Right
KIT GALLOWAY AND SHERRIE RABINOWITZ, *HOLE-IN-SPACE*, 1980. VIEW OF THE BROADWAY DEPARTMENT STORE WINDOW, CENTURY CITY, LOS ANGELES
This pioneering work in telecommunication art used live satellite transmission and high-quality live video and audio to connect unsuspecting members of the public in New York and Los Angeles. Initially described as a 'public communication sculpture', this work became a benchmark and helped set the stage for the development of net art.

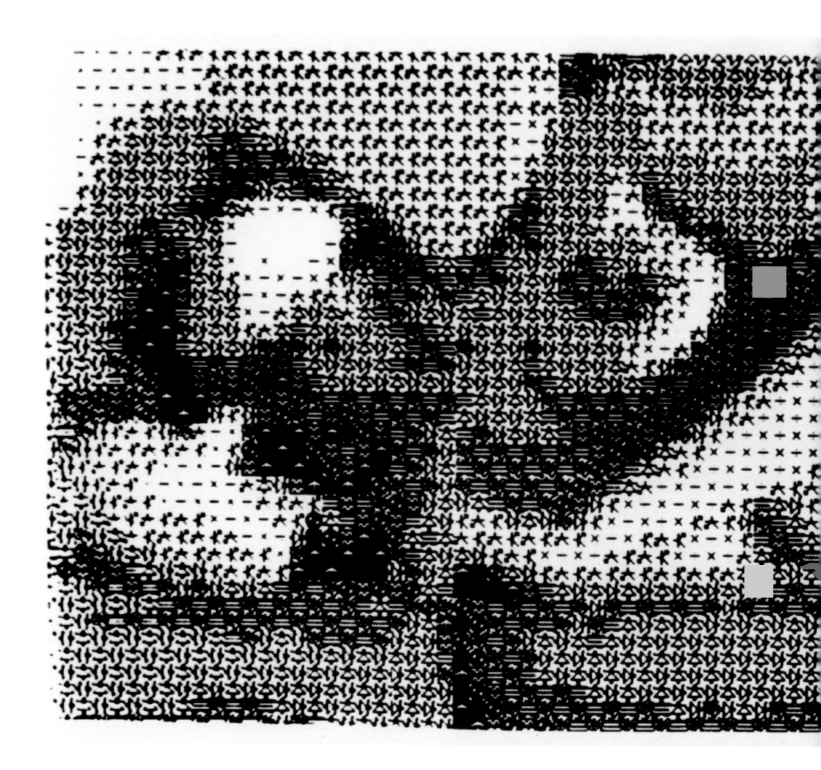

LEON HARMON AND KEN KNOWLTON, *STUDY IN PERCEPTION*, 1966. COMPUTER-GENERATED PRINT, 1.52 X 3.66 M (5 X 12 FT)
One of the most well-known examples of early digital art, this image of a reclining nude was created from 8 frames of 35 mm microfilm using a Stromberg-Carlson 4020 microfilm printer (which produced characters by means of its 'Charactron' tube and vectors). The frames were then printed, abutted, rephotographed and enlarged.

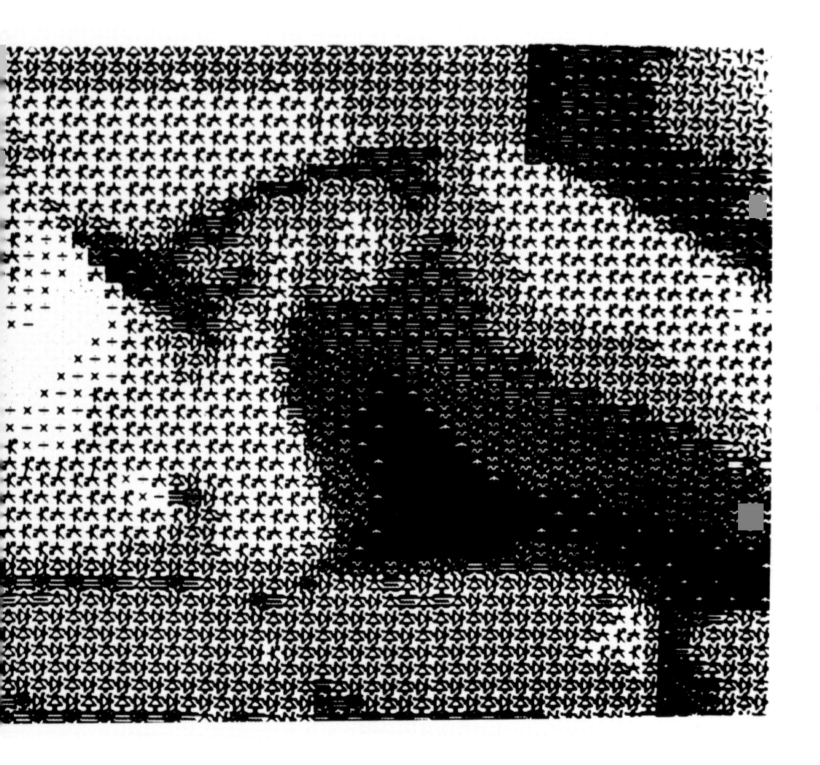

True digital art came into existence shortly after the development of the computer. Following the end of the Second World War, new systems that had been devised for weaponry were adapted for other uses. One result was the invention of the Electronic Numerical Integrator and Computer (ENIAC), based at the University of Pennsylvania, in 1946, which represented the dawn of the digital age. From this point onwards, people began to exploit for aesthetic ends the ability of computers to carry out advanced mathematical calculations.

One of the first to incorporate technology into his artistic practice was Ben Laposky. In the early 1950s he produced electronic images of wave forms on the oscilloscope (a device that uses a cathode ray tube to produce a visual record of an electrical current on a fluorescent screen), which he then photographed. These were complex, mathematically based patterns that could not be drawn by the human hand. Technology was also influencing the world of music and installation: in 1958, Edgard Varèse created his *Poème Electronique* at the World's Fair in Belgium, a sound installation consisting of hundreds of speakers placed in a unique sculptural space designed by the architect Le Corbusier. The work was a foretaste of sound art, and its sound-world consisted of a collage of studio recordings, altered piano sounds, bells and modified recordings of choral music. Both of these examples give an idea of how art and technology were beginning to merge. Much of early experimentation in the aesthetic application of computers was conducted at universities and at the research centres of large companies, such as Bell Laboratories in New Jersey.

The 1960s marked a period of great progress in the development of computer technology – mostly a spin-off of the NASA space programme, which had begun in 1958. The decade also saw increased interest among artists in computer-generated art. In 1966, Leon Harmon and Ken Knowlton created *Study in Perception*, portraying a reclining nude (pp. 22–23). During the 1960s, the American Standard Code for Information Interchange (ASCII) character set was developed to standardize the way in which text data was stored and handled. It consisted of binary code that represented letters, numbers, punctuation marks, symbols and other keyboard functions. ASCII art developed from this code and is still being created today.

Other technological milestones of the late 1960s included the invention of the mouse by Douglas Engelbart in 1968; the frame buffer, which allowed computers to store images for the first time, developed by Bell Labs; and the establishment in 1969 of ARPANET, a localized prototype of the internet – by the United States Department of Defense.

The 1960s also saw a number of seminal exhibitions of computer art at galleries such as the Studiengalerie der TH and Galerie Wendelin Niedlich in Stuttgart, Germany, and the Howard Wise Gallery in New York. In 1966, Billy Klüver established Experiments in Art and Technology (EAT) to encourage interaction between artists and engineers – a group that included Andy Warhol, Robert Rauschenberg, Robert Whitman and John Cage, among others. Two years later, 'Cybernetic Serendipity' debuted at the Institute of Contemporary Arts (ICA) in London and the British Computer Arts Society was founded.

MANFRED MOHR, *P-701B*, 2000. ENDURACHROME INKJET PRINT, CANVAS, WOOD. 141 X 114 CM (55½ X 44⅞ IN)
Considered to be a pioneer of digital art, Manfred Mohr began his career as an action painter and jazz musician. Not satisfied with spontaneous creativity, he turned to more systematic and geometric forms of expression.

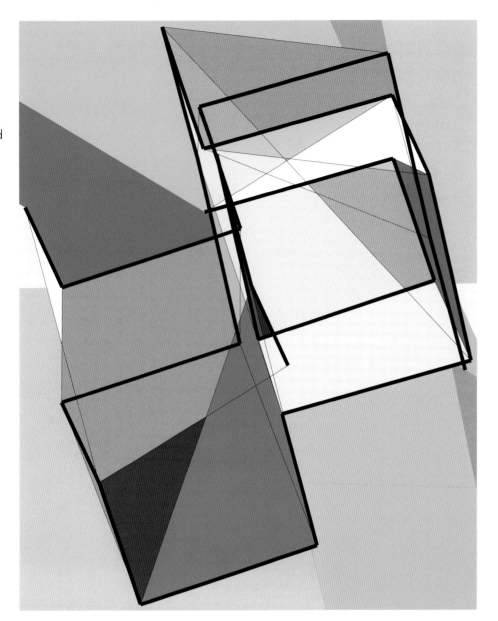

The development of digital art during the 1970s was characterized by artists' continuing exploration of technology. Access to computers was still difficult, and the majority of creative experimentation remained based at research centres, but many building blocks of digital art were nevertheless produced during this period. In 1970, Xerox Corporation established the Palo Alto Research Centre (PARC) at Stanford University in California, with a directive to research computer graphics applications. Also in 1970, General Electric Company introduced Genigraphics, the first high-resolution colour graphics system. Although primarily designed for business graphics applications, it was also used by artists to create high-quality digital images.

While working as a researcher for IBM in 1975, Benoit Mandelbrot developed the concept of fractal geometry, which allowed natural forms to be described through mathematics. The Apple II computer in 1977 brought artists the first personal computer with colour graphics capabilities, and the development of the modem (shorthand for modulator/demodulator) in 1979 enabled the transmission of digital signals over phone lines.

Many prominent professional organizations whose support of the digital arts has been highly influential were founded during this decade. As part of the Association for Computing Machinery (ACM), the Special Interest Group for Graphics (SIGGRAPH) was formed in 1973 and has been at the forefront of developments in computer graphics since its inception. Ars Electronica was established in Linz, Austria, in 1979 to support the development and exhibition of electronic arts, and holds an annual festival that provides a showcase for this work. Thus the 1970s witnessed not only valuable technological advancements for digital artists, but also the beginnings of formal institutional support for digital art.

The following decade was characterized by very rapid advances in the creative uses of computers. Personal computers came into the marketplace and access to digital systems became significantly easier and more affordable. Institutions that supported this development also continued to emerge. The MIT Media Laboratory, founded by Nicholas Negroponte in

1980, involved artists from the time of its conception. The following year, IBM released its first personal computer, which offered artists a machine capable of a limited palette of colours and resolution. With software programmes such as Paintbrush now available, artists could create digital images and output them to slides or paper prints. Adobe Systems was founded in 1982 and remains a leader in digital-imaging software, and the compact disk (CD) was introduced in 1983. Such developments were warmly embraced by those who were creating artwork with digital media. Although the opportunities for exhibiting were still quite limited, artists were increasingly investigating the new creative frontiers offered by these expanding technologies.

During this period, artists also began to focus on telecommunications and animation. One early telecommunications art event was the *Hole-In-Space* project by Kit Galloway and Sherrie Rabinowitz (p. 20), which used a satellite link to enable people in New York City and Los Angeles to interact with each other through life-size video screens. Four years later, Galloway and Rabinowitz co-founded the *Electronic Cafe* (p. 26), another global project designed to link different cultures through telecommunications. Although there was no World Wide Web at that time, a wide variety of other technologies were being employed. *The World in 24 Hours*, organized by Robert Adrian in 1982 and based in Linz, Austria, included groups of artists in fifteen cities around the world who held a series of dialogues through telephone, fax and computer systems.

Computer animation also developed quickly during the 1980s. In Tokyo, *Growth*, the first in a series of computer animations, was created by Yoichiro Kawaguchi in 1983. Three years later Pixar was founded by Steve Jobs of Apple Computers when he purchased the Lucasfilm Computer Graphics Division from George Lucas. Early research at Pixar was extremely important in the development of three-dimensional computer graphics imaging and animation. As animation software became more user-friendly, artists began to experiment more, primarily because it opened up possibilities that had not existed with traditional methods.

Two other major technical innovations came about in 1984: the debut of the Macintosh computer, as mentioned, and the establishment of the Musical Instrument Digital Interface (MIDI). The early Macintosh computers, although offering only black-and-white printing options, ushered in the era of 'desktop publishing'. While the black-and-white pixelated images initially produced were somewhat primitive in comparison with those made by traditional printing methods, artists saw the potential of this new technology. Within the field of music and composition, the advent of MIDI technology revolutionized the music recording industry by making it possible for musicians to own a studio-quality recording system at a reasonable cost.

By 1985, AT&T had developed the TARGA 16 graphics card, which allowed for 16-bit images and 32,000 possible colours. This was a significant development for artists. Although the new card was a considerable improvement, it was not until 24-bit colour was introduced a few years later that computers were able to achieve true photographic

CHAR DAVIES, *TREE POND, OSMOSE,* 1995. DIGITAL STILL IMAGE CAPTURED DURING IMMERSIVE PERFORMANCE OF THE VIRTUAL ENVIRONMENT *OSMOSE.*

Osmose was produced using advanced technology such as stereoscopic 3D computer graphics, spatialized 3D sound and real-time interaction. Participants wear a head-mounted display and a motion-tracking vest that records their breath and balance, enabling them to experience its virtual space. Composed of ever-changing, semi-transparent elements, *Osmose* contains a dozen spatial realms, including a forest, clearing, pond and under-earth, as well as a substratum of software code and upper area of philosophical texts referring to nature, embodiment and technology. *Osmose* was the first virtual environment to employ breath as a means of interface, and to use transparency in real-time. Originally designed to run on a large computer, in 2002 *Osmose* and its successor *Ephémère* were rewritten to run on a PC.

colour resolution and reproduction. To take advantage of this, Adobe developed Photoshop software, which has become an industry standard for image creation and manipulation. These developments in technology, animation and image-making capabilities attracted an even greater number of artists to experiment and create with personal computers.

In 1987, Bernhard Leitner introduced *Head Spaces*, a series of audio sculptures featuring manipulated electronic sounds that were listened to with stereo headphones. In the same year Lillian Schwartz created *Mona/Leo*, which proposed the idea that Leonardo had based the *Mona Lisa* on his own self-portrait. In 1989, Jeffrey Shaw launched *The Legible City*, an interactive environment in which viewers would use a stationary bicycle to navigate around a virtual city, whose 'buildings' were made up of three-dimensional typography. This was one of the first works of art to explore movement through a three-dimensional space that existed solely within the computer.

Educational institutions began to teach computer art on a formal level during this period, and the 1980s ended with the establishment of the first Master of Fine Arts in Computer Art degree programme in the United States at the School of Visual Arts in New York. Books on digital art began to appear. In 1987 *Digital Visions: Computers and Art* by Cynthia Goodman was published in conjunction with an exhibition of digital art at the Everson Museum in Syracuse, New York.

Interest in the digital arts continued to increase throughout the following decade. Computers were now making considerable inroads into creative professions, particularly the field of graphic design. The rapid growth of the internet in the mid-1990s dramatically changed the way in which people communicated and conducted business. The dot.com era not only fuelled the economy, but also introduced new ways in which cultures could interact. A global sensibility was evolving among artists, and the internet was regarded as new creative territory, allowing them to reach international audiences. HyperText Markup Language (HTML) was developed in 1992, paving the way for the World Wide Web. Mosaic, the first example of a graphical web browser, which allowed one to see a combination of text and images while navigating the internet, was released a year later, and the Netscape browser quickly followed. Jodi, the artistic team of Joan Heemskerk and Dirk Paesmans, were among the first artists to experiment with net art. Exhibitions and venues for digital art were also on the rise and, in 1993, the first New York Digital Salon was held at the New York Art Directors Club. Benjamin Weil, Vivian Selbo and Andrea Scott launched äda'web in 1995, an online 'foundry' for artists to experiment with, and reflect upon, the web as a medium.

Interactive art using digital technologies became more prevalent during this period as well. *Sonata*, an interactive cinema work, was created by Grahame Weinbren and Roberta Friedman in 1991 and explored new ways of perceiving cinema. In 1994, Christa Sommerer and Laurent Mignonneau created *A-Volve*, an interactive real-time environment, while Char Davies explored similar virtual reality environments with *Osmose* in 1995 (see above) and *Ephémère* in 1998 (pp. 104–05). This was a very fertile time for digital art, as new creative frontiers were discovered and technology continued to develop at an astonishing rate.

In 1996, John F. Simon, Jr. unveiled *Every Icon* (p. 171), which creates random images based on a 32 x 32 pixel grid – the standard size for computer icons. The unique mathematical nature of this work brought considerable critical attention to net art from the larger art community. Simon also challenged the notion of the conventional art marketplace by selling the work on amazon.com. This piece, and other software and net artworks by artists such as Eduardo Kac (pp. 114–15), Rafael Lozano-Hemmer (pp. 204–05) and John Klima (pp. 31, 132), revolutionized digital art and helped establish its reputation among galleries, museums and curators as a serious art form.

Fuelled in part by the continued rapid development of technology, at the beginning of the 21st century the general public and the international business community were celebrating the rise of the dot.com economy and an international digital cultural boom. The year 2001 brought attention to digital art through several major museum exhibitions in the United States, such as the San Francisco Museum of Modern Art's '010101: Art in Technological Times'. Including both digital and traditional artworks, the show was conceived as an investigation into the effects of technology on our lives. The 'BitStreams' and 'Data Dynamics' exhibitions, both held at the Whitney Museum of American Art in New York, were significant American museum shows of digital art.

New forms of digital art continued to be invented and to push the boundaries of creative expression. Alexander R. Galloway and the Radical Software Group launched Carnivore software, which is based on a surveillance tool used by the FBI to monitor data networks. Innovative forms of performance art also emerged, including *Symphony #2 for Dot-Matrix Printers* written by [The User]. By creating an 'orchestra' of various printers, these artists had a broad palette of sounds with which to compose. Large-scale light installations included Erwin Redl's *Matrix IV* (p. 119), which was exhibited as part of the 2001 Whitney Biennial. Database art was also gaining recognition with *Pockets Full of Memories* by George Legrady (pp. 175–77). This work scanned the pocket contents of gallery visitors and then attempted to identify the objects.

Today, digital art continues to flourish in museums and galleries. It is slowly becoming incorporated into the contemporary art landscape, as many of the perceived differences between digital art and contemporary art become blurred. We are in a period of transition: artists of the future will never have known a world without computers, and are unlikely to distinguish between art created with technology and other types of contemporary art.

JOHN KLIMA, *EARTH*, 2002. NETWORKED SOFTWARE

Earth is a software system that takes data from the internet and visualizes it over a 3D model of the Earth, so that users can zoom in and examine various data layers, such as Landsat 7 satellite images, weather imagery and satellite-mapped topography. The final layer allows users to 'fly' through localized terrain, created by the artist from the upper topographical layer.

DIGITAL IMAGING

We live in a world that is flooded with images of all types from every direction. While people have been making images for thousands of years, digital imaging has a history that is measured only in decades. Despite the genre's newness, however, digital images begin life in a surprisingly large number of ways. They can start as drawings, paintings, photographs or stills from a video, or they can appear as visualizations produced by a computer programme written either by the artist or with commercial software. The final forms these images take can also be very different: they can resemble traditional media, even though digital printing methods have been employed, or they can reside in digital media, such as DVD, CD or the internet. Computer printers can output to a wide assortment of paper types, as well as to canvas, film, fabric and many other media.

Artists who create images using digital technology have at their disposal an expansive range of tools offering new imaging capabilities and a greater control over the creative process, all of which are due to the evolution of sophisticated drawing, painting and image-processing software and the continuing development of powerful computer hardware. The graphics tablet is a good example: while drawing with a mouse is cumbersome and difficult, a graphics tablet today has a pressure-sensitive stylus and software features that emulate not only pencil, pen and brush, but also provide new and completely unique ways of drawing. Some artists prefer to use digitizing tablets to draw or trace images directly into the computer. Others, like Barbara Nessim (p. 67), Kenneth A. Huff (pp. 2, 39) and Lynn Pocock, for example, create traditional sketches that form the basis of their digital works. Viktor Koen (p. 57) combines traditional and digital techniques to create images that achieve a high degree of realism with elements of fantasy. Imaging software has evolved and now offers precise control over every aspect of digital image creation, as well as a host of sophisticated image-processing, automation and output options.

These developments have had a huge impact not only on artists' ways of working, but also on their conceptual and aesthetic approaches. Many continue to create images using traditional methods, incorporating digital elements into the final work. For these artists, digital methods have not displaced but rather augmented their preferred way of creating art. For others, new programming techniques, three-dimensional software and the use of digital output devices have revolutionized the way in which they approach the creative process, leading to the development of a completely new aesthetic.

New digital techniques can be considered as the latest step in an evolutionary process: where traditional drawing and painting methods are constrained by the limitations of physical technique, and photography and video rely on lens-based technologies, digital imaging incorporates elements of mathematical computation and mechanical precision, making possible a whole range of styles from photorealism to pure mathematical abstraction.

The earliest digital printmakers needed to programme the computer before making their drawings because first-generation graphics software did not have an interface. After programming, images were output through the use of plotters – devices that draw pictures on paper with a variety of pens or brushes controlled by digital motors. The use of programming to create images continues to the present day, and artists such as Paul Brown (pp. 44–45), Sherban Epuré (p. 10), Jean-Pierre Hébert (pp. 13, 38), Manfred Mohr (pp. 25, 63), Michael Trott and Roman Verostko (p. 70) all use programming as an integral part of their creative process.

Issues of conservation and archival quality are of great importance for digital printmakers. When colour digital printers were invented, ink and paper were not of archival quality. Many artists were compelled to use photographs from computer monitors, Cibachrome prints or other traditional methods as their final output medium. Unfortunately, a great deal of work that used non-archival printing methods has been lost.

Recent developments in inkjet technology have made it the preferred digital printing method, due to its accurate colour and high-resolution output on a variety of surfaces. A breakthrough in this area was the Iris printer, which sprays ink onto paper affixed to a rotating drum. The images thus produced are named 'giclée' prints, from the French word meaning 'a spray of water'. Although giclée prints have been considered a standard for many years, early versions of the Iris printer used light-sensitive inks, thus compromising the works' stability. One of the pioneers in the area of archival prints is Jon Cone, founder of Cone Editions. Coming from a traditional printmaking background, Cone began experimenting with computers and printmaking in 1984. He was instrumental in refining the giclée process through the development of archival inks, colour management systems and software, first with the Iris and later with Epson printers. His recent innovation, PiezoTone inks, has improved the quality and longevity of black-and-white prints. Today, developments in pigments, inks and papers, as well as the choice offered by other refined printing methods, allow artists to produce high-quality archival images in their digital studios.

This ability to reproduce works at the click of a button has given rise to the question of how we should approach the concept of original prints and editions, so fundamental to printmaking. Some artists choose to print only a single original of a work; many issue limited editions; and others produce open editions. Some artists even provide a copy of the digital file in case an original print should become damaged or faded. All of these practices affect the pricing and availability of digital prints, and to date no standard has evolved.

The digital image maker's studio

Depending on their background and artistic concerns, many digital artists still use traditional image-making tools: pencils, brushes, paints, assorted papers, photographic equipment and so on. They will also have digital work areas, housing the technological components: computer, monitor, scanner, printer, graphics tablet and related peripherals. Computers that specialize in image-making generally have a big monitor, a large amount of random-access memory (RAM) and storage capacity on the hard drive, and a high-performance graphics card. With these features, the artist can choose to create images through photographic manipulation, compositing or freehand drawing with pixel-based software; by plotting points, lines and curves using vector-based software; or by using algorithmic methods or three-dimensional modelling software.

Artists who create two-dimensional images have studios equipped with software packages such as Adobe Photoshop. As the name implies, this software was originally created for working with photographs. Artists can also draw with this application, and it is a primary tool for commercial illustration. Photoshop offers the choice of producing either pixel-based images or vector designs. Files made up of pixels have a specific resolution, and each pixel or dot is assigned a colour. Resolution can be defined as the number of horizontal and vertical pixels contained in an image, e.g. 1024 x 768. Resolution determines the quality of the image; for example, high-resolution files used for printing usually have 300 dpi (300 pixels or 'dots' per inch). Vector images, on the other hand, are defined mathematically. Specific vector-based software packages such as Adobe Illustrator have an advantage over bitmapped (pixel-based) software packages in that they are resolution independent. These programmes use mathematically defined points, curves and shapes to create the image, instead of defining it through a finite number of pixels. The work can be scaled to almost any size without losing quality of line. These imaging methods are by no means exclusive and can be combined in a variety of ways.

Yet another group of digital artists equip their studios with three-dimensional modelling and animation software such as Alias Maya. These programmes offer a tremendous range of options. Unlike two-dimensional systems that work like painting on canvas, where all the elements of light, shadow and perspective are produced through the manipulation of colours, three-dimensional systems create a database that defines all the parameters of the image or object in mathematical space. The artist is able to place cameras, lights and objects into that space, from which the computer renders an image. Charles A. Csuri (pp. 36–37), Kenneth A. Huff (pp. 2, 39), Juan Antonio Lleó (pp. 60, 130–31) and Robert Michael Smith (pp. 68, 97) are among the artists who use this method to create their work. In addition, the final form these files take can be defined by the artist as an image, an animation or even a three-dimensional sculpture, since the data can be saved in a variety of file formats.

Although the works included here represent only a small number of the artists working in digital image-making today, they reflect a variety of styles, from the representational to the abstract, and illustrate diverse approaches and solutions to the integration of computer technologies into existing artistic practice. Ultimately, it will be the task of art historians to help define the impact of digital image-making and its aesthetic concerns on the field of traditional printmaking.

Left
CHARLES A. CSURI, *GARDEN LOVERS*, 1997. INKJET PRINT, 76.2 X 101.6 CM (30 X 40 IN)
A pioneer of computer imaging and animation, Charles A. Csuri creates 3D images that take a variety of final forms. These fragmented figures, constructed entirely of leaves, appear to be dancing in an otherworldly garden.

Below left
CHARLES A. CSURI, *POLITICAL AGENDA*, 1999. CIBACHROME PRINT, 121.9 X 165.1 CM (48 X 65 IN)
Here, a ray-tracing algorithm is used to represent the properties of glass, which appears to distort the objects in the background.

Opposite
CHARLES A. CSURI, *HORSE PLAY*, 1996. INKJET PRINT, 76.2 X 101.6 CM (30 X 40 IN)
These horses are composed of ribbon-like threads that reflect light and cast shadows.

FROM 1965, COMPUTERS REVEALED TO ME A CONCEPT OF CREATIVITY THAT
INVOLVES A HIERARCHICAL PROCESS OF CONTROL. I WORK AT THE TOP LEVEL
USING COMPLEX ALGORITHMS TO DEFINE RULES OR CONDITIONS FOR THE
REALIZATION OF AN IDEA. FOR ME THERE IS NO SINGLE SOLUTION: EACH INSTANCE
OR FRAME IS DIFFERENT. THE IDEAS BECOME ANIMATIONS OR SLIDE SHOWS THAT
COULD RUN UNTIL THE END OF TIME.
CHARLES A. CSURI

I HAVE ALWAYS LOVED TO DRAW. FOR TWENTY YEARS MY PERSONAL ENDEAVOUR HAS BEEN TO CREATE NEW KINDS OF DRAWINGS, WHERE MY MIND OR MY EYES OR MY HAND WOULD NO LONGER BE A LIMIT. DRAWINGS THAT WOULD NOT BE CONSTRAINED BY FATIGUE, CRAMPS, INACCURACIES, DISTRACTION OR THE LIMITS OF TIME. DRAWINGS WHERE NEW LEVELS OF IMAGINATION, PATIENCE, SURPRISE AND DESIRE WOULD BECOME POSSIBLE. I WRITE THE SOFTWARE MYSELF, USING MANY OF THE PARADIGMS FOUND IN NATURE FOR THE CREATION OF SHAPES. THIS IS HOW MY ABSTRACTIONS OFTEN INHERIT THEIR ORGANIC CHARACTER.
JEAN-PIERRE HÉBERT

JEAN-PIERRE HÉBERT, *DIE FORELLE* (DETAIL), 1997. INK ON PAPER, 31 X 23 CM (12¼ X 9 IN)
The algorithms that Jean-Pierre Hébert writes define what he refers to as 'the thread'. That is, a single line that creates complex yet flowing images and gives his work an elegant and lyrical quality.

Left
WONHWA HONG, *VARIATION*, 1993.
DIGITAL PRINT, 52.1 X 69.6 CM (20½ X 27⅜ IN)
This image by Korean–American artist Wonhwa Hong, created using Photoshop, exhibits a very painterly approach to abstract imagery. The patches of colour could almost have been applied with a brush.

Below left
KENNETH A. HUFF, *2002.7*, 2002.
DIGITAL IMAGE, 101.6 X 101.6 (40 X 40 IN)
Below right
KENNETH A. HUFF, *2000.24*, 2000.
DIGITAL IMAGE, 101.6 X 101.6 (40 X 40 IN)
Nature provides much of Kenneth A. Huff's inspiration. He uses photography to gather reference imagery, looking for patterns, forms and unique surface details. Rather than incorporating these photographs into his images, Huff prefers to sketch his ideas and then produce the final work entirely within the software. He was named a 'Maya Master' in 2002 by Alias Systems for his innovative creative work.

THE RANDOM YET STRUCTURED BEAUTY AND MINUTE DETAIL OF NATURE FASCINATES ME AND I REINTERPRET MANY NATURAL PATTERNS AND FORMS IN MY WORK. MY IMAGES ARE OFTEN BASED ON OBJECTS AND SCENES EXPERIENCED IN DREAMS. THE THRILL OF DIGITAL TECHNIQUES IS IN THE ABILITY TO RECREATE THOSE VISIONS IN A PHOTOREALISTIC MANNER. I CREATE IMAGES JUST BEYOND REALITY; THINGS WHICH VERY POSSIBLY COULD EXIST, BUT OBVIOUSLY DO NOT.
KENNETH A. HUFF

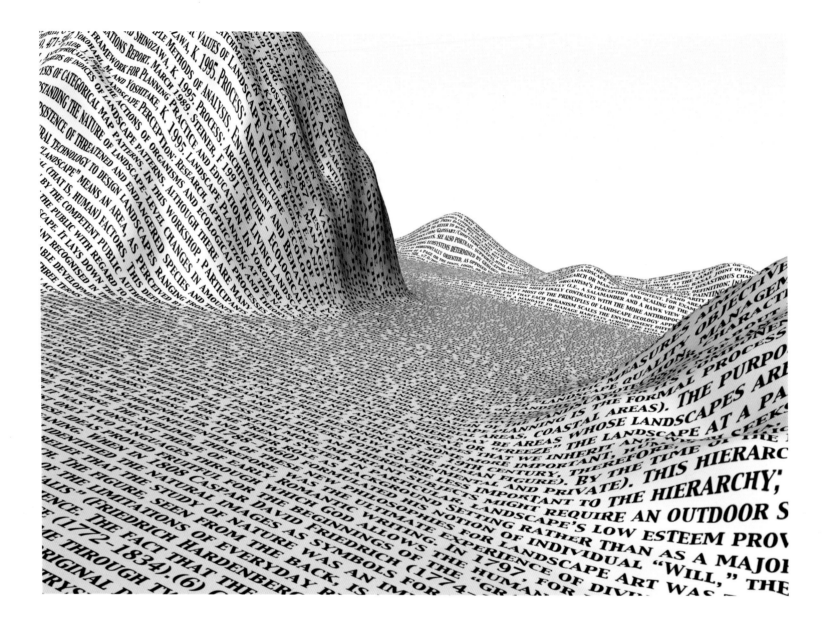

Above
**ROBERT BOWEN, *LITERARY LANDSCAPE*,
2004. DRY ARCHIVAL PRINT,
76.2 X 101.6 CM (30 X 40 IN)**
This piece sits on the border between image-making
and net art, engaging the viewer on visual and
intellectual levels simultaneously. It is part of a series
of images based on the artist's relationship with novels,
personal writings, online texts and translations.

Opposite
**ROBERT BOWEN, *FINNEGAN'S WAKE
(JAMES JOYCE)*, 2004. DRY ARCHIVAL PRINT,
76.2 X 101.6 CM (30 X 40 IN)**
Robert Bowen has used text from James Joyce's novel
Finnegan's Wake to form the substance of this image.
While somewhat abstract from a distance, close
examination reveals an incredibly dense collection
of words.

HERE I EXPLORE MY RELATIONSHIP WITH A VARIETY OF TEXTS. ALL THE IMAGES HAVE ONE THING IN COMMON: THEY ARE CREATED WITH TYPOGRAPHICAL SYMBOLS AND THEY FUNCTION BOTH AS PICTURES AND AS TEXTS. ULTIMATELY, FOR ME THEY ARE VIRTUAL IMAGES OF VIRTUAL THINGS.

ROBERT BOWEN

Above
**VICTOR ANDERSON, *TIME,* 2002.
DURST LAMBDA PRINT, 60 X 180 CM
(23⅝ X 70⅞ IN)**
Although this work is based on a photograph,
digital manipulation of the image has introduced
a sense of motion.

Left
**VICTOR ACEVEDO, *ERIC IN ORENSE,* 2000.
DIGITAL PRINT, VARIABLE DIMENSIONS**
This is a portrait of the artist's brother Eric. Victor
Acevedo's work explores the structure of
contemporary space by imposing 3D matrices onto
images taken from everyday life.

MY WORK USES PHOTOGRAPHY BUT IS COMPUTER-BASED, AS THE FINAL IMAGES ARE CREATED AND DEVELOPED IN THE DIGITAL REALM. MOREOVER, IT IS THE COMPUTER-GENERATED COMPONENT THAT IN FACT DRIVES THE WORK'S PRIMARY PURPOSE. MY INTENTION IS TO CARRY FORTH IN THE TRADITION OF METAPHORIC AND GRAPHIC SPATIAL REPRESENTATION EVIDENT AT THE HEART OF THE HISTORY OF PAINTING.

VICTOR ACEVEDO

Above
PAUL BROWN, *SWIMMING POOL*, 1997.
GICLÉE PRINT, 50 X 75 CM (19¾ X 29½ IN)
Paul Brown is concerned with the concepts of artificial life
in both his prints and his time-based work. By using
algorithmic processes, he generates abstract images that
involve the viewer through their complex and rhythmic
patterns. The title of this work and its overall colour and
rippling lines, are strongly suggestive of the shapes and
forms that exist in water.

Opposite
PAUL BROWN, *GYMNASTS*, 1997.
GICLÉE PRINT, 60 X 80 CM (23⅜ X 31½ IN)
Not knowing in advance what a work will look like, Paul
Brown titles the works retrospectively, sometimes alluding
to other artists' work (*Swimming Pool* refers to David
Hockney), thus illustrating his belief that computational
art continues the tradition of art-making. Here he uses
a less cryptic reference: the dominant figures remind him
of gymnasts wearing black leotards.

MY WORKS ARE BASED IN A FIELD OF COMPUTATIONAL SCIENCE CALLED CELLULAR AUTOMATA OR CAs. THESE ARE SIMPLE SYSTEMS THAT CAN PROPAGATE THEMSELVES OVER TIME AND BELONG TO THE DISCIPLINE KNOWN AS ARTIFICIAL LIFE OR A-LIFE. I HAVE BEEN INTERESTED IN CAs AND THEIR RELATIONSHIP TO TILING AND SYMMETRY SYSTEMS SINCE THE LATE 1960s. RATHER THAN BEING CONSTRUCTED OR DESIGNED, THESE WORKS 'EVOLVE'. I LOOK FORWARD TO A FUTURE WHERE COMPUTATIONAL PROCESSES LIKE THE ONES THAT I BUILD WILL THEMSELVES MAKE ARTWORKS WITHOUT THE NEED FOR HUMAN INTERVENTION.

PAUL BROWN

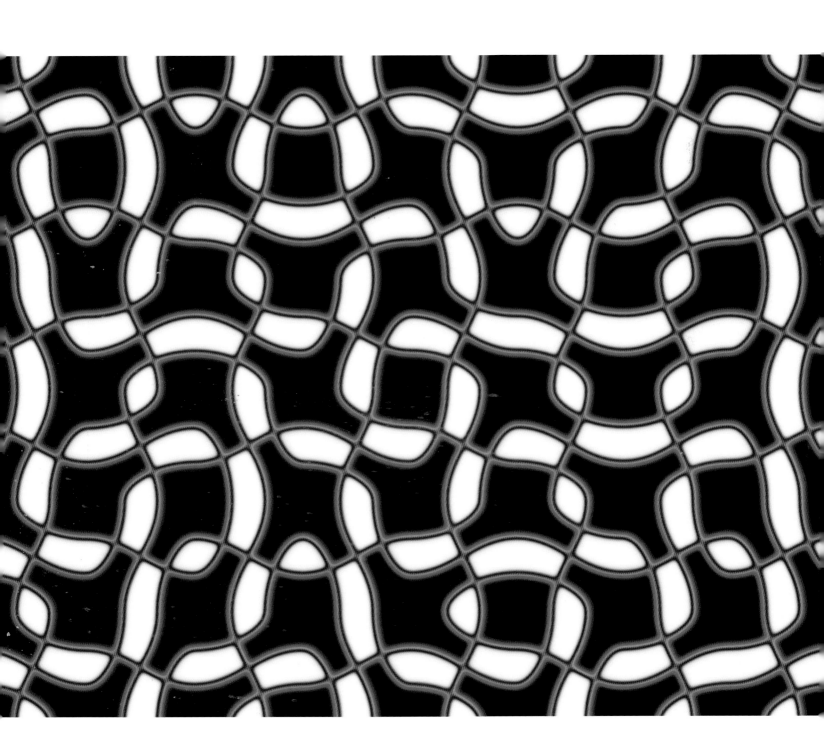

DIGITAL ART HAS GREATLY AFFECTED HOW I CREATE AND THINK ABOUT MY WORK. I SEE MY WORLD IN PIECES. I CONCEIVE OF IDEAS THAT I WILL EVENTUALLY VISUALIZE USING THESE PIECES. IT IS THIS CREATIVE PROCESS THAT AFFORDS ME A METHOD OF WORKING.
DENA ELIZABETH EBER

Above
DENA ELIZABETH EBER, *CONVERSATIONS 1*, 2000.
DIGITAL IMAGE, 54.6 X 76.2 CM (21½ X 30 IN)
Conversations is a series that explores family lineage and relationships by means of visual juxtapositions. In this image, the artist illustrates the first conversations she had with her unborn daughter. The series is part of a larger body of work, *Aitz Chayim*, which means 'The Tree of Life' in Hebrew and symbolizes growth, motherhood, strength, life, immortality and rebirth.

Opposite
ROBIN DOHERTY, *UNTITLED 1*, 2001.
DIGITAL PRINT, 76.2 X 76.2 CM (30 X 30 IN)
While the media Robin Doherty works in range from photography to sculpture and installation, his main concern is with the search for self-knowledge. Some of the adjectives he uses to describe his work are 'metaphysical', 'meditative', 'intuitive' and 'iconic'. His concern with the iconic is evident in the focused gaze of this child's face.

THE MOST IMPORTANT EFFECT THAT THE DIGITAL PROCESS HAS HAD FOR ME IN RESPECT OF MY ART PRACTICE IS THAT IT HAS GIVEN ME THE FREEDOM TO PLAY BEYOND SET BOUNDARIES. THE USE OF THE WORD 'PLAY' BY NO MEANS SUGGESTS A NON-SERIOUS OR TRIVIAL INFERENCE: PLAY IS FUNDAMENTAL TO ALL ART AND IN THE DIGITAL PROCESS WE HAVE FOUND AN IMPORTANT AND EXCITING FORM OF THIS, GIVING NEW POSSIBILITIES OF SUCH A FLUID AND DYNAMIC NATURE THAT ITS IMPORTANCE CANNOT BE OVERSTATED.
ROBIN DOHERTY

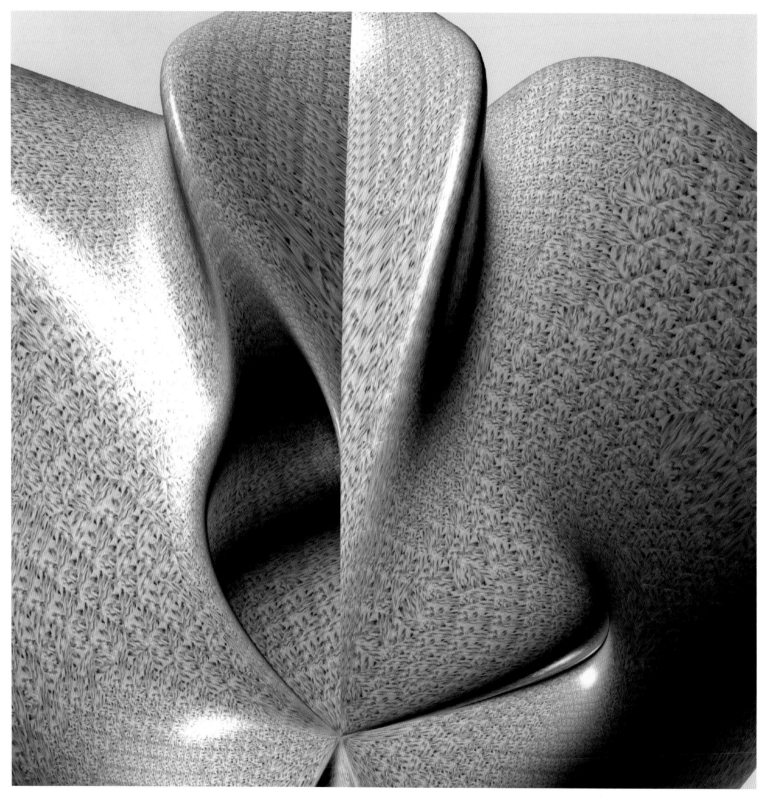

WHEN I FIRST BEGAN TO USE COMPUTERS, IDEAS CAME UP THAT WOULD NOT HAVE OCCURRED TO ME OTHERWISE, AND THE IMAGES BEGAN GROWING INTO AND OUT OF EACH OTHER. EVENTUALLY I WAS ABLE TO USE THE COMPUTER INTUITIVELY, AND AS THE TOOL BECAME MORE TRANSPARENT TO ME, I BEGAN TO EXPLORE THE UNIQUE QUALITIES OF THE COMPUTER AS AN ART MEDIUM.

DAVID EM

Opposite
DAVID EM, *GUADALUPE*, 1998. COMPUTER GRAPHICS IMAGE, VARIABLE DIMENSIONS

Left
DAVID EM, *GLACIER*, 1997. COMPUTER GRAPHICS IMAGE, VARIABLE DIMENSIONS
David Em is a pioneer of digital imaging, having first worked with computers in 1975 with the Superpaint programme at the Xerox PARC research facility.

MANY OF MY PIECES HAVE REFERENCES, ECHOES, TO THE THEATRE AND OTHER LITERARY, ARTISTIC AND SCIENTIFIC IDEAS AND PHILOSOPHIES. SPECIFICALLY, I AM FASCINATED BY THE WORK OF THE SURREALISTS – RENÉ MAGRITTE AND SALVADOR DALÍ – THE IDEA OF *TROMPE L'OEIL* PAINTING, OF TIME, SPACE AND RELATIVITY, CHAOS THEORY AND, OF COURSE, THE CLASSICAL THEATRE OF THE GREEKS. WHERE THIS WILL TAKE ME I AM NOT SURE – BUT I LOOK FORWARD TO THE JOURNEY.
JOHN CAMPBELL FINNEGAN

JOHN CAMPBELL FINNEGAN, *TEMPORAL DISTORTION*, 2002. GICLÉE PRINT, 91.4 X 182.9 CM (36 X 72 IN)
John Campbell Finnegan creates images that are abstract and fluid. His work combines photography, painting, collage and scanned 3D objects.

MY WORK DERIVES TECHNICALLY FROM TWO DIFFERENT MEDIUMS: FROM THE COMPUTER, WHICH I FIRST LEARNED AS A GRAPHIC DESIGN TOOL, AND FROM PHOTOGRAPHY, WHICH OPENED A SURPRISING NEW REALM OF MEANING FOR MY WORK. I WAS ABLE TO FIND MY OWN VOICE AND TO CREATE PERSONAL LANDSCAPES FROM IMAGES THAT COMPELLED ME TO PHOTOGRAPH THEM.
DIANE FENSTER

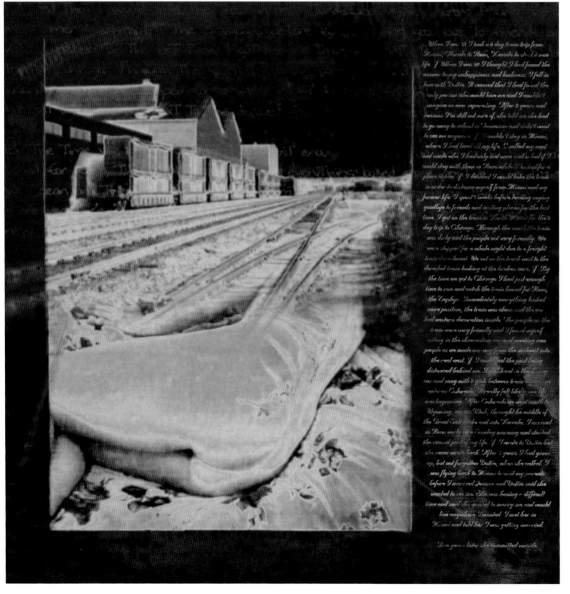

Left
DIANE FENSTER, *I COULDN'T STAY IN MIAMI*, 1994. FUJICHROME SUPERGLOSS PRINT, 76.2 X 76.2 CM (30 X 30 IN)
This image is from the series *Ritual of Abandonment*, which explores the emotions of love, abandonment and relationships through the intermingling of images and text. A term Diana Fenster uses to describe her work is 'psychological narrative'. In 2001 she became the first artist to be inducted into the Photoshop Hall of Fame. Fenster's work is a combination of still video, photography, video and scanned imagery. She also creates installations that incorporate her imagery (p. 106).

Opposite
TAMÁS F. FARKAS, *CELTIX-4*, 2003. DIGITAL GRAPHIC, 42 X 29.7 CM (16½ X 11⅝ IN)
Tamás F. Farkas uses the computer as a design tool. Influenced by multi-dimensional geometry and abstract symmetries, as well as the works of M. C. Escher, his works are dissymetric in their construction, with the intent of forming a final composition from individual elements.

Left
SUE GOLLIFER, *UNTITLED G1*, 2000.
GICLÉE PRINT, 48.2 X 48.2 CM (19 X 19 IN)
By exploiting the uncertainty, rapidity and chaotic nature of computation, Sue Gollifer looks for unexpected results that will provide solutions to artistic problems and invite new discussions about the relationship between artist and viewer.

Below left
DONA J. GEIB, *REMNANTS OF THE SOUL*, 2003. DIGITAL PRINT AND ENCAUSTIC ON WOOD PANEL WITH METAL AND GOLD LEAF, 45.7 X 45.7 CM (18 X 18 IN)
Dona J. Geib started working with digital methods in 1976, having been a traditional printmaker up to that point. She now uses digital cameras to gather the source images for her works, which she then combines and reshapes using digital technology before they are output as digital prints and further elaborated.

Opposite
LAURENCE GARTEL, *CONEY ISLAND BABY*, 1999.
INKJET PRINT, 147.3 X 182.9 CM (58 X 72 IN)
With a background as a photographer and videographer, Laurence Gartel began experimenting with video synthesizers and digital images in the mid-1970s. He was one of the first artists to explore digital imaging and photo manipulation. Gartel's works are inspired by visits to particular places, but then assume layers of complexity as he manipulates them into their final form.

NEVER IN THE HISTORY OF THE WORLD HAVE WE SEEN SUCH CHANGES IN THE WAY OUR SOCIETY RECEIVES AND PROCESSES INFORMATION. OUR THOUGHTS AND METHODOLOGIES ARE EVOLVING ALMOST ON A 'REAL TIME' BASIS. AS AN ARTIST WHO HAS WORKED IN THE ELECTRONIC MEDIUM FOR OVER THIRTY YEARS I HAVE WITNESSED MANY OF THESE CHANGES FIRST-HAND.
LAURENCE GARTEL

Left
ISAAC KERLOW, *BLUE PEARL*, 1998. INKJET PRINT, 27.9 X 83.8 CM (11 X 33 IN)
Coming from a background in traditional printmaking, in the 1980s Isaac Kerlow began to explore the possibilities of combining these techniques – etching, engraving and silkscreen – with computer-generated imagery.

Opposite
HELEN GOLDEN, *MOLTEN ELEMENTS*, 1999. MIXED-MEDIA, 73.6 X 53.3 CM (29 X 21 IN)
Helen Golden can be described as a traditional artist who uses digital tools. She feels that the addition of technology to her artistic repertoire has given her a more immediate access to her imagination, thereby enhancing her creative process.

I AM NOT ATTRACTED TO THE COMPUTER BECAUSE OF ITS ABILITY TO CREATE PERFECTION OR PURE GEOMETRY. MY INTEREST IN COMPUTERS IS TO GENERATE EMOTIONAL WORKS WITH A GESTURAL, UNPOLISHED QUALITY TO THEM.
ISAAC KERLOW

***MOLTEN ELEMENTS*, WHICH EXPLORES THE EMERGENCE OF A LIFE-FORCE AS EMBODIED BY THE TWO FIGURES, IS PART OF A SERIES OF IMAGES ABOUT RELATIONSHIPS. I SCANNED A WOODCUT PRINT AND SEVERAL PHOTOGRAPHS OF A POSING COUPLE, ONE OF A NILE SUNSET AND ONE OF LIGHT STREAKS FROM FLARES. USING COMPUTER ART-MAKING APPLICATIONS I COLLAGED AND PAINTED THE DIGITIZED INFORMATION.**
HELEN GOLDEN

CHRIS S. JOHNSON, *TECHNODARHMA*, 2003. INKJET PRINT AND ACRYLIC TRANSFERRED ONTO WOOD, 50.8 X 33 CM (20 X 13 IN)

This image references classical Buddhist art and symbolism while introducing contemporary elements such as a mobile phone, a PDA and an aerosol can. Chris S. Johnson's work combines an illustrative approach with the creative possibilities of imaging software. Although there is a playful element to his work, it also comments on the primary role technology has assumed in contemporary society.

I EXPLORE THE BOUNDARIES OF OBJECT AND COMPUTER IMAGERY. THE INITIAL CREATION OF THE IMAGE IS NOT THE ENDING POINT: AFTER PRINTING IT GOES THROUGH A SERIES OF MANIPULATIONS OF MEDIUM AND FORM. THE FINAL OBJECT IS FAR FROM ITS INITIAL EPHEMERAL FILE BUT HOLDS HIDDEN TRUTHS TO BE EXPLORED BY THE VIEWER.

CHRIS S. JOHNSON

A FUSION OF SCULPTURAL ELEMENTS, WEAPONS AND ARMOUR, THESE 'VICTORY' COMPOSITIONS HAVE HISTORICAL ROOTS IN WORKS LIKE *THE NIKE OF SAMOTHRACE* AND DELACROIX'S CELEBRATED PAINTING *LIBERTY LEADING THE PEOPLE*. ELEMENTS AND DETAILS WERE JUXTAPOSED DIGITALLY FOR A SEAMLESS, ALMOST PAINTERLY FINISH, TRADITIONAL IN ITS LOOK, IF UNORTHODOX IN CONTENT. THE DAMSELS' FACES WERE SELECTED FROM 1940s AND 1950s COMMERCIAL PHOTOGRAPHY, ANOTHER ERA WHEN TRUTH WAS GLAMORIZED FOR MASS CONSUMPTION.
VIKTOR KOEN

VIKTOR KOEN, *DAMSEL NO. 6* AND *DAMSEL NO. 15*, FROM THE SERIES *DAMSELS IN ARMOR*, 2002. ARCHIVAL PRINTS ON CANVAS, 89 X 61 CM (35 X 24 IN)
When looking at Viktor Koen's work, one is compelled to stop and re-examine it closely. While the most modern digital tools were used to create the images, there is a sense that they might be paintings from a previous century. These works are a commentary on the brutality of war, portrayed through creative and masterful uses of technology.

Far left
LINDA LAURO-LAZIN,
***ARTIFACTS*, 1995.**
DIGITAL PRINT, 28 X 21.6
(11 X 8½ IN)
This image, part of Linda Lauro-Lazin's *Pixels and Sticks* series, combines natural forms with pixilated patterns. The artist began using digital technology in 1986.

Left
BONNY PIERCE LHOTKA,
***FENCELINE*, 2003.**
INKJET ON PHOTO PLATE,
81.3 X 61 CM (32 X 24 IN)
With a background in printmaking and painting, Bonny Pierce Lhotka began her digital art explorations with an Apple II computer in 1982, initially to create black-and-white plates for block printing. This rich and colourful work is part of the *Aerial Essence* series, created with photographs taken from airplane windows and framed by a collection of objects from junkyards and flea markets.

SEEING THE WORK IS A VISUAL AND COGNITIVE EXPERIENCE WHICH EXPLORES OUR MOVEMENT, OUR STEREO-VISION AND OUR UNDERSTANDING OF SPACE AND DEPTH. DESPITE THE COMPLEXITY AND APPARENT CHAOS OF THESE THREE-DIMENSIONAL DRAWINGS, THERE ARE SIMPLE RULES THAT ORGANIZE THEM.
TONY LONGSON

Below left and right
TONY LONGSON, ***CHEETOS*,**
1978–86. SCREEN PRINT ON
PLEXIGLAS (WITH DETAIL),
121.9 X 121.9 X 15.2 CM
(48 X 48 X 6 IN)
This work is formed by the relationship between patterns printed on layers of Plexiglas – achieved through Longson's use of rotational symmetry.

Opposite
DOROTHY SIMPSON
KRAUSE, ***REFLECTIONS*,**
2003. INKJET PRINT ON
ALUMINIUM, 61 X 61 CM
(24 X 24 IN)
Dorothy Simpson Krause began her art career as a painter and collage-maker and started working with computers in the late 1960s. She received the Smithsonian Technology in the Arts Award for organizing 'Digital Atelier: A Printmaking Studio for the 21st Century' at the National Museum of American Art in 1997.

BY FOCUSING ON TIMELESS PERSONAL AND UNIVERSAL ISSUES – HOPES AND FEARS, WISHES, LIES AND DREAMS, IMMORTALITY AND TRANSIENCE – I CHALLENGE MYSELF AND THE VIEWER TO LOOK BEYOND THE SURFACE TO SEE WHAT DEPTHS ARE HIDDEN. I IMBUE MY WORK WITH THE QUALITY OF ALLEGORY.
DOROTHY SIMPSON KRAUSE

Above
JUAN ANTONIO LLEÓ,
GEOMETRA 6P8C, **2000–01.**
INKJET PRINT ON KODAK PAPER,
45 X 60 CM (17¾ X 23⅝ IN)
This work is from a collection of abstract images that
were created using the Asymetrix Web 3D software.
Juan Antonio Lleó is also known for his installation,
musical and multi-media work, as well as for his
collaborative projects (pp. 130–31).

Opposite
HILARY LORENZ, *CELLULAR STUDY 3,* **1999.**
C-PRINT MOUNTED ON PLEXIGLAS,
53.3 X 175.3 CM (21 X 69 IN)
Hilary Lorenz here explores medical, scientific and
pseudo-scientific elements side by side. In so doing,
she invites us to consider the relationship between art
and science.

TO DEFINE A COMPLEX SYSTEM THAT GENERATES SOUND OR IMAGES AND MODULATE IT TO PRODUCE INTERESTING RESULTS, AND THEN COMBINE IT WITH OTHER ELEMENTS OR USE IT AS THE STARTING POINT FOR A NEW PROCESS, IS A KIND OF GAME THAT I LOVE TO PLAY. UNDOUBTEDLY, THE COMPUTER IS A PERFECT PARTNER FOR THIS. I THINK OF MY IMAGES AS ABSTRACT PICTURES IN MOTION, CHANGING, BUT NEVERTHELESS SIMILAR TO THEMSELVES.
JUAN ANTONIO LLEÓ

THE TENSION BETWEEN ADDRESSES THE CONFLICT BETWEEN OPPOSING FORCES. WHEN THE IDEALS OF TWO ENTITIES CLASH, THE DISHARMONY CREATES A NON-PHYSICAL SPACE THAT ENGULFS BOTH PARTIES. BETWEEN THE PIERCING ANGER OF ATTACK AND THE CONVICTION OF ONE'S OWN BELIEFS, AN EXCLUSIVE, TRANSITORY WORLD IS CREATED. THIS OFFENSIVE YET CAPTIVATING SPACE OF VULNERABILITY AND STRENGTH HELPS TO ESTABLISH OUR INNER VOICE AND DEFINE OUR DIRECTION IN LIFE.
BONNIE MITCHELL

Above left
BONNIE MITCHELL, *THE TENSION BETWEEN*, 2000. INKJET PRINT, 76.2 X 106.7 CM (30 X 42 IN)
Bonnie Mitchell created this image using 3D modelling, particle systems and dynamics software. The artwork contains contrasting red and green elements that appear to consume and intermingle with amorphous yellow shapes. The textures have been created using digital photography manipulated in Photoshop and mapped onto the surface of the geometry.

Above right
MAUREEN NAPPI, *WELDED CHAMBER*, 2003. VIRTUAL THREE-DIMENSIONAL PAINTING, VARIABLE MEDIA AND DIMENSIONS
Maureen Nappi's work is elegant, refined and complex. She combines a variety of techniques to make artwork that focuses on the relationship between humanity and technology, spiritualism, feminism and race. An advocate of new forms of art, Nappi was instrumental in creating a funding category for computer arts within the New York Foundation for the Arts.

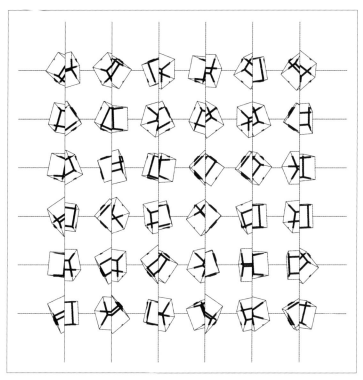

I WRITE COMPUTER ALGORITHMS, I.E. RULES THAT CALCULATE AND THEN GENERATE A WORK THAT COULD NOT BE REALIZED IN ANY OTHER WAY. IT IS NOT NECESSARILY THE SYSTEM OR THE LOGIC I WANT TO PRESENT IN MY WORK, BUT THE VISUAL INVENTION THAT RESULTS FROM IT. MY ARTISTIC GOAL IS REACHED WHEN A FINISHED WORK CAN VISUALLY DISSOCIATE ITSELF FROM ITS LOGICAL CONTENT AND CONVINCINGLY STAND AS AN INDEPENDENT ABSTRACT ENTITY.
MANFRED MOHR

Above left
MANFRED MOHR, *P-197K*, 1977. PLOTTER DRAWING, ACRYLIC INK ON CANVAS, 183 X 183 CM (72 X 72 IN)
In this example of Manfred Mohr's creative explorations, cubes are divided into two parts by one of the Cartesian planes. Each element of the split cubes is rotated independently, creating a broken symmetry. The final image is composed of an array of cubes in a 6 x 6 matrix.

Left
NANCY MCGEE, *CHROMOSCOPE SHIELD*, 2000. 78-TILE EPSON ARCHIVAL INKJET PRINT, 228.6 X 152.4 CM (90 X 60 IN)
Symmetry and pattern play an important role in Nancy McGee's work. This image from her *Survival Series* consists of seventy-eight vividly coloured genetic maps.

CYNTHIA BETH RUBIN,
THE WILDER BUILDING,
ROCHESTER, NY, 2002.
DIGITAL PAINTING,
VARIABLE DIMENSIONS
The Wilder Building has special
meaning for the artist, as it was
where her father began his law
practice. The combination of
painting, digital collage and
architecture is prevalent in
Cynthia Rubin's interpretive work.
Trained as a painter in the era
of abstraction, she also works in
web art, interactive installation
and virtual reality.

MY WORK IS AN INVESTIGATION OF THE THREADS OF CULTURAL MEMORY, THAT I FEEL BOTH FROM MY OWN VISUAL EXPERIMENTS AND THROUGH THAT MYSTERIOUS TRANSMISSION OF SENSIBILITY THAT COMES FROM SOME PLACE BEYOND THE INDIVIDUAL. I AM INTERESTED IN HOW CULTURAL TRADITIONS COLLIDE AND MERGE, AND HOW THIS IS EMBEDDED IN ALL OF US.
CYNTHIA BETH RUBIN

JOSEPH NECHVATAL, *VIRAL COUNTER-ATTACK*, 2003. SCREEN CAPTURE, VARIABLE DIMENSIONS

Highly theoretical in his approach, Joseph Nechvatal creates large robot-assisted paintings on canvas and makes use of viral processes to develop the imagery. The dark areas on the left and right of this screen capture show the virus affecting the image.

JAN PAMULA, *IMAGE 019A*, 2001. DIGITAL PRINT, 50 X 60 CM (19¾ X 23⅝ IN)

Jan Pamula is an example of a painter and printmaker working with geometric abstraction who made a smooth transition to working in the digital realm. Geometry and colour form the structural basis of his work.

I WANT MY AUDIENCE TO EXPERIENCE THE INTIMACY OF THE FORMS AND TEXTURES I HAVE PHOTOGRAPHED OR DRAWN, AND TO EXPERIENCE MY FASCINATION WITH DETAIL, COMPLEXITY AND REPETITION. IN THIS ERA OF BEING WIRED, I WANT MY WORK TO SERVE AS AN OASIS OF CALM, AN INTROSPECTIVE RETREAT. MY WORK IS INTENDED TO BE UPLIFTING, A JOYFUL OBSERVANCE OF NATURAL FORMS TRANSFORMED INTO ICONS FOR MEDITATION AND CONTEMPLATION.
KARIN SCHMINKE

KARIN SCHMINKE, *FORM:INFORM*, 2004.
DIGITAL/MIXED-MEDIA TRIPTYCH,
61 X 182.9 CM (24 X 72 IN)
Karin Schminke draws her inspiration from the forms and patterns of nature. She works with mixed-media, combining photography, drawing and printmaking with digital techniques to produce images that suggest the power and mystery of the natural environment.

BARBARA NESSIM, *HAND MEMORY*, 1986. FUJIX COLOUR DIGITAL PRINT ON PAPER, 76.2 X 61 CM (30 X 24 IN)

Barbara Nessim comments that this piece was conceived after watching a television programme on prehistoric cave-paintings. She states, 'The programme made me wonder how far we have come, cave paintings to electronic art. *Hand Memory* addresses that thought.'

ROBERT MICHAEL SMITH,
JOGAE DENTATA, **1999.**
DIGITAL PRINT ON CANVAS,
182.9 X 121.9 CM (72 X 48 IN)
Robert Michael Smith works in both sculpture and
2D digital imaging. This large-scale print shows his
continuing exploration of archetypal forms based
on the structures of nature.

JAVIER ROCA, *X/Y MACHINA*, 2000.
INKJET PRINT, 190.5 X 114.3 CM (75 X 45 IN)
X/Y Machina is a metaphor, a composite conceived
to explore the idea of the perfect female/male body.
The body is recomposed through layers of fragmented
imagery, suggesting analogies between the human and
the mechanical and revealing our desire to manipulate
our own genetic heritage.

**LILLIAN SCHWARTZ, *FLOWER 1A*, 2000.
DIGITAL PRINT, VARIABLE DIMENSIONS**
Lillian Schwartz was one of the first digital artists to
exhibit her work, which appeared in 'The Machine
as Seen at the End of the Mechanical Age' at the
Museum of Modern Art, New York, in 1968. Her
contributions to the analysis and restoration of art
using digital technology have been widely
recognized, specifically in the field of Italian
Renaissance painting. *Flower 1A* is one of a series
of frames created with palettes to be viewed with
ChromaDepth™ 3D glasses. This series is a
continuation of her interest in the study of colour
and visual perception that began in the 1960s
with the late scientists Leon Harmon and Bela Julesz.

**SERGIO SPADA, *EVOLUTION*, 2000.
DIGITAL PRINT, 101.6 X 71.1 CM (40 X 28 IN)**
Sergio Spada's abstract geometric constructions in
empty space have a solidity that equates them with
some examples of virtual sculpture.

Below
ROMAN VEROSTKO, *CYBERFLOWER IV, GOLD VERSION*, 2000. ALGORITHMIC PEN-AND-INK DRAWING ON PAPER, 58.4 X 73.6 CM (23 X 29 IN)
One of the pioneers of algorithmic art, Roman Verostko has worked for more than twenty years with programming and pen plotters to create intricate and beautiful digital drawings. His interest in electronic art started in the 1960s, and he first began to experiment with algorithmic art twenty years later. Verostko is interested in creating what he calls 'form generators' and is influenced by the early 20th-century artists Mondrian, Kandinsky and Malevich.

Opposite
JOAN TRUCKENBROD, *ARTIFICIAL FRAME*, 1994. GICLÉE PRINT, 55.9 X 71.1 CM (22 X 28 IN)
Much like the process of revealing and concealing sacred symbols that are painted on one's body during a ceremony and visible in the flickering of firelight at night, Joan Truckenbrod's artwork uses light and the flow of colour fluids to sculpt the ecology of social environments.

ANNA URSYN, *MONDAY MORNING*, 1995. PHOTOSILKSCREEN/ PHOTOLITHOGRAPH, 61 X 81.3 CM (24 X 32 IN)

In this work, Anna Ursyn addresses the issues of daily cycles, multiplicity and narrative. Rather than relying on the idea of a single image, she repeats and reframes various motifs, encouraging the viewer to see things from several perspectives. The title of this image plays on the concept of the weekly work routine.

WHAT EXCITES ME IS THE CONTINUING CONVERGENCE BETWEEN PAINTING, PHOTOGRAPHY AND THE DIGITAL. THE PROCESSES, TECHNIQUES AND SOFTWARE CAN BE SO RICH AND SURPRISING I SOMETIMES FEEL LIKE STANDING BACK AND LETTING THE PICTURES MAKE THEMSELVES WITHOUT ANY INTERFERENCE FROM ME.
JAMES FAURE WALKER

JAMES FAURE WALKER, *F-G THE RESTLESS INVENTOR OF CINEMA*, 2000. IRIS GICLÉE PRINT, 50.8 X 71.1 CM (20 X 28 IN)

This image is from the series *Colour & Motion*. James Faure Walker approaches his art from the perspective of a painter, having started to integrate digital techniques into his work in 1988. Walker maintains separate studios for each discipline.

I USE THE COMPUTER AS AN ARTISTIC TOOL, SIMILAR TO A BRUSH, TO REALIZE, EXPLORE AND CREATE IMAGERY THAT HAS CONTINUED TO INTEREST ME AS AN ARTIST THROUGHOUT MY PROFESSIONAL CAREER.
MICHAEL WRIGHT

MICHAEL WRIGHT, *THE LIGHT*, 1992. DIGITAL PRINT, 121.9 X 152.4 CM (48 X 60 IN)

In his creative work Michael Wright attempts to reveal the spiritual force behind surface appearances. He works with video and portraiture in low resolution to capture a sense of immediacy.

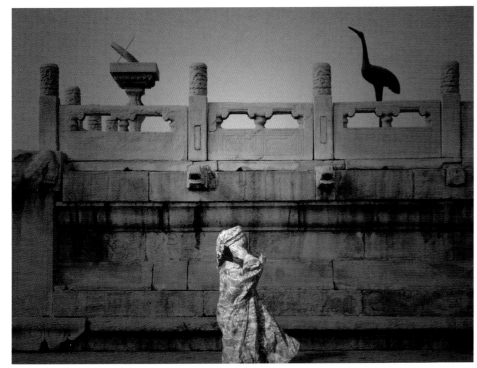

LIU WEI, *FORBIDDEN CITY SERIES NO. 1*, 2000. DIGITAL IMAGE, 33 X 45 CM (13 X 17¾ IN)

With the Forbidden City in Beijing as the backdrop for this series of digitally altered photographs, Chinese artist Liu Wei illustrates the indelible history such scenes suggest, coupled with his childhood memories of the shadow puppet theatre. His many photographic series compare and contrast the past with the present, revealing the symbolic meaning contained within the images.

Below
MARK WILSON, *PSC31*, 2003. ARCHIVAL INKJET PRINT, 119.4 X 88.9 CM (47 X 35 IN)
Coming from the background of a traditional artist who explored abstract and geometric imagery, Mark Wilson began working with computers and developing his own software in 1980. His early digital work focused on mapping pixels onto complex geometric structures. Wilson continues to develop his software, using both random and geometric techniques.

Opposite
BRUCE WANDS, *BUDDHA LIGHT PAINTING #4*, 2004. INKJET PRINT, 48.2 X 33 CM (19 X 13 IN)
The *Buddha Light Paintings* series is based on the geometric shapes and proportions that underlie Buddhist art, the rules of which date back several thousand years. Historical templates were scanned and brought into 3D software, creating abstract visual interpretations while preserving the original spiritual intent.

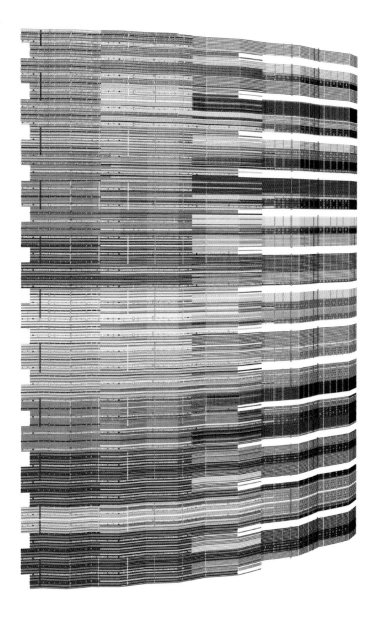

BECAUSE OF THEIR UNIQUELY DIGITAL NATURE, THESE PICTURES ARE UNREALIZABLE WITH OTHER METHODOLOGIES. RATHER THAN DISGUISING PIXELS, I HAVE MADE THEM THE CENTRAL ELEMENT OF MY ART-MAKING. SINCE THE EARLY 1970s I HAVE BEEN DEEPLY INVOLVED WITH ABSTRACT DRAWING AND WITH THE ELABORATION OF COMPLEX LINEAR IMAGES.
MARK WILSON

DIGITAL SCU LPTURE

The origins of digital sculpture can be traced back to the first practical applications of computers. Initially, computing was employed mainly in the areas of military defence and in computer-assisted drawing (CAD) and computer-assisted manufacturing (CAM), and the technologies were adapted early on for use by the aerospace and automobile industries. As modelling/animation software and hardware developed, their potential application in the field of digital sculpture became apparent.

As with most early computer technologies, artists had difficulty gaining access to the equipment. Nonetheless, they fully recognized the opportunities this medium presented and, even before facilities to fabricate digital sculpture were available, sculptors began to explore the use of three-dimensional software to design their sculptures and the new creative possibilities that it offered. Part of the appeal of these early computer simulations was that artists could create and visualize forms that were free from the natural constraints of weight, size or gravity: they could make three-dimensional works that were limited only by their own imagination. CAD/CAM also spawned computerized numerical control (CNC) milling and rapid prototyping, with which industrial designers and sculptors can make physical models of objects from three-dimensional software files. These technologies have since become affordable, and sculptors can now submit a three-dimensional digital file to a service bureau and have a physical model fabricated.

Sculptor Rob Fisher's interest in working with digital technologies (p. 92) sprang from a desire to see what different forms he could invent. While Fisher embraces the use of the computer in creating his work, he also continues to use traditional techniques, stating that 'In my latest artwork, I have in some ways come "full circle" and returned to traditional studio techniques, augmented, however, by the use of the computer. One should use the computer when it is appropriate: to save time or to permit development of forms that would otherwise be difficult by virtue of their complexity, engineering or scale.'

Some artists use digital technologies both in the design and in the physical creation of their works; some design on screen but adhere to

traditional methods of production; and others make sculptures that exist only in the virtual realm in the form of a three-dimensional model, image or animation. A number of works give no clues that they were produced using digital means, whereas others exhibit an intricacy or distortion that could have only been produced with a computer.

Sculptors using purely traditionally techniques begin by sketching and drawing their ideas from a variety of perspectives while developing the concept. When the drawings have been completed, models and maquettes are created in various sizes in order to refine the original concept. These creative experiments eventually evolve into the finished work. The choice of material clearly has an impact on the production process, since the sculpture might be carved from stone or cast from metal or other media. By using a computer, however, the artist can avoid the considerable costs involved in producing prototypes or, indeed, the final works themselves: the ability to make refinements in the digital realm gives artists the flexibility to embark on projects that may otherwise have been simply too complicated or expensive to take beyond the conceptual stage.

Virtual sculptures are created with three-dimensional modelling software and consist of a database of numbers that defines their shape, volume and surface properties. Many software applications to create digital sculpture are available, Alias Maya being one of the most sophisticated. First, the sculptural objects are created and visualized in a 'wire frame' mode, to which surfaces are then applied in the form of a 'skin'. Sculptors examine their work from any viewpoint and select from a wide variety of surface properties – such as stone, metal and plastic or any other material – all of which can be applied or changed quickly and easily. They can also modify the look of the sculpture immediately as they work, which aids in its conceptual development. If a sculptor had to execute these drawings and visualizations by hand, it would take a considerable amount of time and require significant rendering skills on the part of the artist. Many digital sculptors admit that the computerized design process can be as time-consuming as its traditional counterpart, but note that by using the computer as a visualizing tool they can dedicate much more time to refining their ideas.

The ability to create a three-dimensional object in cyberspace offers the sculptor tremendous scope. With physical constraints lifted, forms can take unique and complex shapes. Surface properties, such as colour, texture and reflectivity, can also be further manipulated and are not, as in physical sculpture, limited to the chosen material. Since the sculptural file resides in a computer, it can be sent to and accessed from remote locations over the internet. Sculptors can also use photo-imaging software to modify photographs and 'insert' their sculpture in a wide variety of environments – a substantial advantage when designing site-specific installations.

One of the first sculptors to use three-dimensional software was Kenneth Snelson (pp. 86–87), who explored this area in the early 1990s. Snelson's sculptures incorporate the interplay of tension and compression, reflecting his embrace of the mathematical concept that he calls 'tensegrity'. Snelson likens his sculptures to musical compositions in which the elements interact

and resonate with each other. Bruce Beasley (pp. 80–81) and Rob Fisher, artists who had long championed the use of computer technologies by sculptors, initiated public discussion of the potential offered by digital technologies at the 1990 International Sculpture Center's biennial conference in Washington, DC. The interest generated by the conference led to the establishment of the Computers and Sculpture Foundation (CSF), a group that continued the discussion on the use of computer tools in the making of sculpture. The CSF was founded by Bruce Beasley, Timothy Duffield, Rob Fisher and David Smalley.

A few years later, at the Inter-Society for the Electronic Arts (ISEA) conference in 1995, Ars Mathematica, an organization in France, also promoted the use of digital technology for sculpture and presented the programme 'Computer Sculpture in the USA and France'. This was followed by the 'INTERSCULPT '95' exhibition and an accompanying videoconference that linked the Silicon Gallery in Philadelphia with the Galeries Graphes in Paris, and the dialogue among digital sculptors continues today on www.sculpture.org. Christian Lavigne (p. 93), a sculptor and the organizer of the INTERSCULPT conference, talks about his work this way: 'For a poet of shapes, new technologies give perfect tools to materialize the "creative verb". It is the first time in human history that writing and describing an object turn from virtuality to reality.'

The digital sculptor's tools and methods
While traditional techniques are still employed by many sculptors, digital tools have opened up whole new areas of creativity. Depending on the individual artist, the studio at first glimpse may look like a traditional sculptor's atelier, albeit with the addition of a computer. Most artists continue to outsource the prototyping of three-dimensional models and also rely on printouts of images and drawings for reference.

The process of creating sculpture, be it physical or virtual, using digital means begins with the inputting, scanning and visualization of information – technology that evolved from developments in the commercial arena, such as medical imaging and industrial manufacturing. Several methods of importing data exist. Once an object has been scanned into the computer, it can be refined, modified or 'virtually sculpted'. This is the most creative part of the sculptor's experience. Although the data compiled through scanning provides the basic form and proportions of the object, allowing the computer to display it as a wire-frame construction, it is the three-dimensional software that gives the artist complete control over how the object looks, its size and what the surface properties will be. While modifications are mostly executed with a mouse and keyboard in the usual fashion, one significant development was the invention of the haptic input device – a type of interface that calculates the density of the virtual material inside the computer and transmits tangible feedback to the artist, allowing him or her to feel and shape the virtual surface in the way a sculptor using traditional material might mould clay.

For artists creating a virtual sculpture, the completed work exists as a data file. The final virtual form can be output as a variety of file types or

media, including two-dimensional prints; QuickTime VR files, which allow one to see the sculpture from any viewpoint; interactive three-dimensional files for virtual reality environments; or they can be part of a movie or animation. Those sculptors who want a physical object prepare a digital file to output via a computer-controlled manufacturing machine. The result can be either the finished sculpture itself or a mould from which the sculpture is cast.

Among the early technologies developed to manufacture sculptures and moulds were CNC milling machines. The CNC process is a subtractive one and its advantages include a high degree of accuracy, the potential for creating large-scale objects, and lower cost when compared to rapid prototyping. One of the foremost sculpture studios in the eastern United States is the Johnson Atelier (recently renamed the Digital Atelier and Sculpture Foundation Studio) in New Jersey. Originally a traditional foundry, it now offers both traditional and digital production methods for sculptors. The studio can mill from expanded polystyrene (EPS) foam, wood, glass and certain types of wax and plastic, and has the capacity to fabricate objects up to 3 x 3 x 1 metres in size (10 x 10 x 5 feet). Larger works can be built in small sections and assembled later. Close by is the Digital Stone Project, which took over the Johnson Atelier Stone Division in 2003.

Alongside CNC milling is the technique of three-dimensional printing, which uses powder–binder technology. In this process, a thin layer of powder that is slightly larger than the cross-section of the desired object is spread onto a surface. The printer then sprays a liquid binder – in the exact shape of the object's cross-section – onto the powder, thus creating a solid layer. The liquid binder is repeatedly sprayed on in thin layers until the final sculpture is built up in three-dimensional form. This method is generally referred to as rapid prototyping and has the advantages of allowing undercuts, nested elements, interior voids and lattice-like structures that are impossible with conventional CNC milling. Although primarily used for industrial design and manufacturing, these printers are also capable of creating objects with almost limitless colour choices and offer extraordinary possibilities to the sculptor.

As can be seen, the integration of art and technology is prevalent in the realm of the digital sculptor. A technical understanding of the potential that these technologies bring to the tool set is necessary, both for an appreciation of its impact on the future development of this art form, as well as to gain new perspectives on its aesthetics.

The physical and virtual artworks that follow include creations by many of the pioneers of digital sculpture. As sculptors continue to explore digital technologies, new forms and structures, as yet unimagined, will emerge.

I HAVE BEEN USING THREE-DIMENSIONAL DIGITAL MODELLING TO CREATE MY SCULPTURES SINCE 1987. I USE IT LIKE A THREE-DIMENSIONAL DRAWING PAD THAT ALLOWS ME TO WORK ON THE SCULPTURE FULLY IN THE ROUND, BUT VERY SPONTANEOUSLY. WHEN MODELLING DIGITALLY, I CAN SAVE INTERESTING ACCIDENTS OR NEW IDEAS THAT DEVELOP AND RETURN TO THEM LATER AS THE BEGINNING OF A NEW PIECE.
BRUCE BEASLEY

Opposite
**BRUCE BEASLEY, *BREAKOUT*, 1991. CAST BRONZE,
71.1 X 111.8 X 30.5 CM (28 X 44 X 12 IN)**

Above left
**BRUCE BEASLEY, *OUTREACH*, 1998. CAST BRONZE,
104.1 X 71.1 X 25.4 CM (41 X 28 X 10 IN)**

Above right
**BRUCE BEASLEY, *INSURGENT*, 2001. CAST BRONZE,
127 X 63.5 X 45.7 CM (50 X 25 X 18 IN)**

Bruce Beasley's sculptures are based on the geometric shapes that he
creates with his computer. Those shown here are cast in bronze, although
he has also worked in cast iron, aluminium, acrylic and wood. Beasley
maintains that he would produce the same type of sculpture with or
without the computer, but recognizes that the computer allows him to work
more quickly and intuitively. Rather than spend enormous amounts of time
building physical models, he instead uses the software to refine his ideas.

SUZANNE ANKER, *ORIGINS AND FUTURES*, 2004. RAPID PROTOTYPE SCULPTURES, PYRITE AND STAINLESS STEEL, INSTALLATION, VARIABLE DIMENSIONS

Suzanne Anker works in a variety of media and addresses the relationship between art and genetics. In this mixed-media installation, rapid prototype sculptures of embryos, 3D Rorschach inkblot images and other abstract forms reside among pieces of pyrite on a steel table.

DAN COLLINS, *SPEAKING LIKE ADULTS*, 1993–2003. MIXED MEDIA, 110.5 X 243.8 X 91.4 CM (43½ X 96 X 36 IN)

The focus of this work is an exact half-scale likeness of Dan Collins's mother set at one end of an anamorphically distorted table. The data set for the head was captured using a Cyberware 3D laser digitizer. The model of this head was subsequently rendered in proprietary software, and then cut using a CNC mill. A silicone mould was used to create a hollow head, which was then painted with acrylics and completed with a wig made from natural mohair. This juxtaposition between reality and virtuality is at the heart of Collins's creative approach.

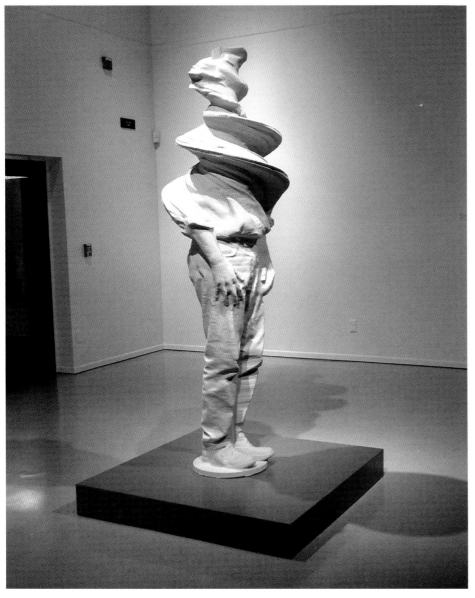

DAN COLLINS, *TWISTER*, 2003. CNC-MILLED URETHANE, 243.8 X 76.2 X 76.2 CM (96 X 30 X 30 IN)

This sculpture is a self-portrait. The data set was generated in 1995 using a Cyberware full-body laser scanner. The artist stood on a turntable that was spun by his wife. The movement captured during the initial part of the scan produced the distorted results; by the time the scanner reached his waist, he had stopped spinning. The data was then output to a custom CNC milling machine to create the final sculpture.

DAN COLLINS, *RETURN TO THE GARDEN*, 2003. NETWORKED VIDEO INSTALLATION, CNC-CUT WOODEN PARTS, NETWORKED COMPUTER, PRINT, MONITOR. ROOM SIZE APPROXIMATELY 3.7 X 9.1 X 9.1 M (12 X 30 X 30 FT)

At first glance, this installation appears to be a chaotic assemblage of black silhouettes. When one looks at the camera view, either on the internet or on the laptop in the gallery, the video images resolve into landmark moments from mythology and the history of flight. They include silhouettes of Icarus, Otto Lilienthal, the Hindenburg, the Space Shuttle Challenger, a Boeing 767 and a Blackhawk helicopter. Viewers can select a series of 'presets' that direct the camera to the images. Dan Collins's intention is for viewers to question the truth of images, the power of machines and the seduction of handmade objects.

MY CURRENT SERIES OF WORK UTILIZES COMPUTER MODELLING TO CONTROL THE KIND AND DEGREE OF DISTORTION IMPOSED ON A GIVEN OBJECT OR DATA SET. SCALING OPERATIONS, PROPORTIONAL SHIFTS, ECCENTRIC VANTAGE POINTS, MORPHING PROCESSES AND THREE-DIMENSIONAL MONTAGE ARE SOME OF THE TECHNIQUES EXPLORED BY THIS BODY OF WORK. PART OF THE CHALLENGE HAS BEEN TO GET FORMS 'OUT OF THE BOX' (THE COMPUTER) AND FULLY REALIZED IN AN ACTUAL, TANGIBLE FORM. I AM INTERESTED IN THE GAP BETWEEN THE VIRTUAL SPACE OF THE COMPUTER AND THE TANGIBLE, BODY-FELT REALITY OF SCULPTURAL OBJECTS.
DAN COLLINS

Left
KENNETH SNELSON, *STAR LANDING*, 1990. DIGITAL PRINT, 76.2 X 95.3 CM (30 X 37½ IN)

Below left
KENNETH SNELSON, *FOREST DEVILS' MOON NIGHT*, 1990. DIGITAL PRINT, 76.2 X 95.3 CM (30 X 37½ IN)

Opposite
KENNETH SNELSON, *CHAIN BRIDGE BODIES*, 1991. DIGITAL PRINT, 76.2 X 101.6 CM (30 X 40 IN)
Kenneth Snelson is one of the most well-known and influential contemporary artists working with sculpture, mathematics and photography. His early interest in Constructivism and geometric art led him to study with Buckminster Fuller at Black Mountain College in 1948. This experience clarified his aesthetic concepts and he began to incorporate principles of tension and compression into his work rather than follow Fuller's fascination with pattern and structure. Having worked mainly with mathematics early in his career, he made a smooth transition to the use of computers. The works shown here are some of the earliest examples of virtual sculpture.

MY ART IS CONCERNED WITH NATURE IN ITS PRIMARY ASPECT, THE PATTERNS OF PHYSICAL FORCES IN THREE-DIMENSIONAL SPACE.
KENNETH SNELSON

ANNA URSYN, *HERO HORSE*, 1989. COMPUTER-ENHANCED SCULPTURE, 63.5 X 53.3 X 78.7 CM (25 X 21 X 31 IN)
Anna Ursyn's work explores the relationship between the human and animal worlds, juxtaposing natural environments (such as the forest floor shown here) with man-made constructions, and incorporating carefully manipulated prints on paper and canvas into the final structures.

FIRST, I SKETCH A GENERAL OUTLINE FOR THE COMPOSITION, AND THEN I DRAW ABSTRACT GEOMETRIC DESIGNS AS A STARTING POINT FOR THE EXECUTION OF MY COMPUTER PROGRAMMES. THE WIRE-FRAMED THREE-DIMENSIONAL DESIGNS GUIDE CONSTRUCTION, WHILE IMAGES – MULTIPLIED, SUPERIMPOSED, TRANSFORMED – OFFER THE ILLUSION OF TIME AND MOVEMENT. I USE THE VISUAL LANGUAGE OF THESE PROGRAMMES TO SHOW AN IMAGE OF THE HORSE AS A HEROIC SYMBOL OF THE HUMAN STRUGGLE FOR SURVIVAL.
ANNA URSYN

PETER TEREZAKIS, *SOUND BLINKER*, 1983. WEARABLE ELECTRONIC SCULPTURE, 5 X 5 CM (2 X 2 IN)

This small pin incorporates circuitry both as an aesthetic element and to control the LEDs that blink in response to sound or conversation. It forms part of a series that he began in 1976, when he designed a small LED pin for actress Claudette Colbert.

JAMES SEAWRIGHT, *ORION*, 2002. DIGITAL INTERACTIVE SCULPTURE, METAL, PLASTIC, ELECTRONIC COMPONENTS, 30.5 X 30.5 X 25.4 CM (12 X 12 X 10 IN)

James Seawright began making electronic sculptures in the 1960s, working with analogue circuitry, some of which originated from electronic music processes. One of the attractions for Seawright was the potential for interaction between the work, various environmental factors and viewers. By the mid-1970s, he became involved with microprocessors and built digital circuits to control his interactive sculptures.

JAMES SEAWRIGHT, *HOUSE PLANTS*, 1984. DIGITAL INTERACTIVE SCULPTURE, METAL, PLASTIC, ELECTRONIC COMPONENTS, APPROX. 152 X 152 X 61 CM (5 X 5 X 2 FT)

House Plants, an early example of cybernetic botany by pioneer James Seawright, was composed of electronic 'plants' that exhibited robotic behaviour in response to changing light levels and other stimuli. The 'petals' moved up and down, and lights on the plants were programmed to flash in various patterns.

MY RECENT WORK CONTINUES AN INTEREST IN AESTHETIC CONCERNS AGAINST CONCEPTS OF ARTIFICIAL LIFE ... WHETHER THE ORGANISM IS SUCCESSFUL IN A NATURAL SENSE IS IRRELEVANT. THE PIECES ARE PUSHED TO PERFORM THEIR MOTION REGARDLESS. THE ANIMATIONS TAKE PLACE IN A NO-SPACE, AN INFINITELY BANAL AND NEUTRAL SPACE. DESPITE THE PERFUNCTORY PERFORMANCE OF THEIR ACTIVITY, THE WORKS TAKE ON SUGGESTIVE PSYCHOLOGICAL NUANCES. ONE HAS MULTIPLE COMPLEX RESPONSES DESPITE THE CLEAR UNDERSTANDING THAT THE WORKS ARE UNREAL, FABRICATED AND CONSTRUCTED.
MICHAEL REES

Opposite
MICHAEL REES, *PUTTO8 2X2X2X2 V2*, 2003.
RESIN-FILLED PLASTER, 3D PRINT, HAMMERED METAL PAINT,
39.4 X 55.9 X 43.2 CM (15½ X 22 X 17 IN)

Above
MICHAEL REES, *PUTTO8 2X2X2X2*, 2003. PAINTED
FIBREGLASS, 198.1 X 157.5 X 182.9 CM (78 X 62 X 72 IN)
Michael Rees's sculptures begin life as computer models created with
3D modelling/animation software and are then made into physical
sculptures, animations or prints. Rees calls his virtual digital sculptures
'meta-forms', meaning that the end result can take on a variety of forms
or be produced in different media. These works are composed of body
parts that have been reconfigured into artificial life forms.

Below left

ROB FISHER, *PROTOS*, 2001. STAINLESS STEEL, ALUMINIUM, 4.6 X 4.6 X 4.9 M (15 X 15 X 16 FT)

This work was inspired by a round doorway in an ancient garden in Suzhou, China. Rob Fisher describes it as 'exploring relationships between container and contained, between the simple but primal character of the circular spiralling form and the complex complementary sculptural elements within'. The central element is kinetic and is moved by the power of the wind. Both digital and traditional methods were used in its design and construction: the central form was fashioned from styrofoam, while the helical form was rendered using 3D software.

Below right

ROB FISHER, *DIHEDRALS*, 2002. ALUMINIUM FLAGPOLE MASTS, STAINLESS STEEL NET AND RIGGING, ALUMINIUM KINETIC ELEMENTS, 7.6 X 9.1 X 9.1 M (25 X 30 X 30 FT)

Dihedrals (named after the geometric shape used to describe winged objects such as birds and planes) is a large-scale kinetic sculpture designed to sway and shimmer in the wind. Rob Fisher used both CAD and engineering software to calculate the structural properties of the sculpture and to ensure that it was capable of withstanding hurricane-force gales.

CHRISTIAN LAVIGNE, *L'AGE DU FER*, 2002. CRYSTAL 3D LASER ENGRAVING, 10 X 10 X 12 CM (4 X 4 X 4¾ IN)

Christian Lavigne, a pioneer of digital and virtual sculpture, is credited with producing the first piece of rapid prototype sculpture in France, in 1994. Lavigne is typical of many digital artists in that he has a diverse background including science, mathematics, poetry and art. He co-founded Ars Mathematica, an international group of artists that promotes new technologies in sculpture, in 1992, and three years later co-founded 'INTERSCULPT '95', a worldwide biennial for interactive and simultaneous digital sculpture. This image is a 3D laser engraving produced in a block of crystal. Lavigne combines geometric shapes with figurative elements to create complex yet delicate constructions.

CHRISTIAN LAVIGNE, *CYBERSALY 3: LE SECRET DE L'ETRE*, 2002–03. SLS POLYAMIDE, 33 X 34 X 26 CM (13 X 13⅜ X 10¼ IN)

This intricate bust, pierced through and enveloped in ribbon-like contours, could only have been reproduced using rapid prototyping techniques.

MARK MILLSTEIN, *FREQUENCY KITE 2,* **2003. INKJET ON MULBERRY PAPER, BAMBOO, STRING. 61 X 45.7 CM (24 X 18 IN)**

Mark Millstein began to design kites as a way to 'get the digital image out of the frame' and to unite computer-designed images with sculpture and handwork. 'The partnership of digital design and printing with the activity of folding and gluing paper, and cutting and bending bamboo, is a contemplative combination that is particularly fulfilling', he states.

Left and below
DAVID CURT MORRIS, *RAINMAKER*, 2001. KINETIC WATER SCULPTURE, HEIGHT 13.7 M (35 FT)
Sculptor David Curt Morris uses water as an integral part of his work. He often employs 3D images and computer animation when planning projects in order to give an accurate rendition of what a sculpture will look like and how it will function.

IT IS NOW POSSIBLE FOR AN INDIVIDUAL DESIGNER TO INCREASE PRODUCTION SPEED BY SIMULATING A TEAM THAT WOULD ACCOMPLISH MODELLING, ENGINEERING AND PRESENTATION. THE INVESTIGATIVE PATHWAY HAS BEEN WIDENED FOR AN EXPLORATION OF MATHEMATICAL FORMS, WHICH WAS IN THE PAST AN ARDUOUS JOURNEY. IT IS NOW POSSIBLE TO DREAM AND CONFIRM ALL IN THE SAME SETTING.
DAVID CURT MORRIS

WHERE OTHERS WORK WITH CLAY OR CARVE MARBLE, I USE ZEROS AND ONES, SHOWN AS PHOSPHORESCENT ELECTRONS ON A MONITOR, TO CREATE EPHEMERAL FORMS THAT ARE LATER FABRICATED INTO SOLID SCULPTURES. THE DIGITAL SCULPTURES ARE CREATED ON POWERFUL PCs WITH CAD SOFTWARE. THEY ARE THEN HANDCRAFTED AND MOULDED. THE FINAL SCULPTURE IS FABRICATED OF A MATERIAL CREATED BY NASA FOR THE SPACE SHUTTLES AND THEN HAND-DIPPED INTO AUTOMOBILE LACQUER DOZENS OF TIMES UNTIL THE SMOOTH WHITE FINISH IS ACHIEVED.
CORINNE WHITAKER

Below left
CORINNE WHITAKER,
NEW BEGINNINGS, 2001.
DIGITAL SCULPTURE

Below right
CORINNE WHITAKER,
SCULPT 1.3.00D, 2000.
VIRTUAL SCULPTURE
Best known for her 'blobs' –
sensuous, organic forms – Corinne
Whitaker uses both virtual and
physical sculpture to invent a new
visual and geometric language.

Opposite above
ROBERT MICHAEL SMITH,
EPHESIANCYBERGIN, 2003.
CNC-CUT MARBLE,
45.7 X 61 X 45.7 CM
(18 X 24 X 18 IN)

ART IS ALCHEMY. ALCHEMY IS THE MAGIC, OBSERVATION, PROCESS AND RITUAL OF LIFE. MY SCULPTURES, BOTH VIRTUAL AND ACTUAL, ARE CONVERSATIONS REGARDING THE ARCHETYPAL FORMS THAT ARE THE BASIC STRUCTURES OF NATURE. I BUILD ALIEN ABSTRACT WORLDS THAT BECOME FAMILIAR THROUGH FREQUENT IMMERSION. THESE WORLDS ARE CONSTRUCTED TO OPEN EXPLORATION TO THE DEEPEST REGIONS OF THE HUMAN PSYCHE FOR DEVELOPMENT WITHIN THE LANDSCAPE OF THE IMAGINATION.
ROBERT MICHAEL SMITH

Opposite below
ROBERT MICHAEL SMITH,
GYNEFLEUROCERAPTOR,
2003. **CNC-CUT MARBLE,**
61 X 45.7 X 45.7 CM
(24 X 18 X 18 IN)
The forms created by Robert
Michael Smith in both his sculptural
work and prints exhibit a strong
biomorphic quality. Smith, who has
been involved with digital sculpture
since the early 1990s, uses CNC
milling to reproduce the whorls
and curves of organic shapes in
the traditional medium of marble.

DIGITAL INST ALLATION A ND VIRTUAL REALITY

Installation and virtual reality art have evolved from the fields of architecture, sculpture and performance. Before museums and galleries allowed general access to works of art, gathering places such as churches and public squares offered almost the only opportunities for the general public to come face to face with works of art. The palaces and grand domestic architecture of wealthy patrons provided early venues for artists to create highly aesthetic environments.

However, it is in the early 20th century that installation art truly has its roots, specifically in the art movements of Futurism and Dada. Founded in Italy in 1909, Futurism embraced the products of the Industrial Revolution – noise, speed, machines and technology – and celebrated change, innovation and originality. The Futurists' call for the merging of art and science, as well as the integration of media, formed some of the building blocks of digital installation art. The philosophy and innovations of the Dada artists were even more influential as forerunners of digital installation and virtual reality art. Dadaism broke down the boundaries that separated different art forms from one another and from everyday life, and heralded the concepts of appropriation, performance art and audience participation, and further set the stage for immersive experiences. During this period the very nature of the art object was undergoing radical change. Marcel Duchamp's 'ready-mades' demonstrate both the appropriation of objects as art and the acknowledgment of the participation of the viewer, providing the conceptual and aesthetic basis for many artists who became interested in installation as an art form and leading directly to the Conceptual Art and Anti-Art movements of the 1960s.

The emergence of video art accelerated an interest in digital installation. While early video art focused on content, on what was being shown, artists such as Nam June Paik soon began to use television sets as sculptural elements. Paik's pioneering work in sound and video during the late 1950s and early 1960s paved the way for his later video sculptures and installations. As new video technologies became available, artists were quick to use them for their creative projects. The evolution of videotape into the videodisk format spawned two early digital installation artworks of importance. In 1979 Lynn Hershman Leeson created *Lorna*, a tale about an agoraphobic woman who never leaves her apartment. Viewers could control the interactive video's storyline with a remote control much in the same way as the main character, and the plot had multiple variations that were randomly accessed. This allowed the audience to form what Leeson described as a 'metaphorical link' with the protagonist. *Erl King*, another early videodisk work, created in 1983 by Grahame Weinbren and Roberta Friedman, prompted viewers to move between multiple story lines. Both examples show how artists were approaching the concept of interactive cinema, but primarily from the point of view of controlling plot and narrative. Over the decades, these pioneers and such notable artists as Woody and Steina Vasulka, Bill Viola and Tony Oursler have continued to push the boundaries of this art form.

The creative possibilities of interactivity and the development of immersive environments were both given a large boost by the arrival of computers in installation art, which allowed artists increased control over the interactive experience and access to cyberspace and virtual worlds. Early interactive artworks were produced through custom-made electronic circuits. The hardware and the computer programming required were both expensive and difficult to configure. Today, off-the-shelf software packages such as Cycling '74 Max/MSP and Macromedia Director can control a variety of devices, both digital and analogue. These packages allow programmers to customize computer code for specific needs and also to transfer this code to small microprocessors that can be easily concealed within an installation.

The term 'immersive environments' is applied primarily to virtual reality works, although it is also used to describe other kinds of digital installations, such as those featuring video projection or interfaces that surround the participant. Virtual reality brings the user into a total digital environment by means of (usually) three-dimensional graphics and multi-channel, spatialized sound. This is normally accomplished through the use of a head-mounted display and data glove, or, in the case of virtual reality environments such as the Cave Automatic Virtual Environment (CAVE), through a surround-screen, surround-sound video projection system. The internet has also provided new possibilities in installation art, including remote-controlled cameras, sensors and other devices. 'Telematics' is the term used to define the combination of computers and telecommunications networks. It should be remembered that although the computer has had an enormous influence on this type of creative work, there continues to be no clear-cut distinction between analogue and digital installation art. Installation artists simply use whatever technology is available to them, or whichever they prefer, to further their artistic endeavour, and a host of interfaces has been developed by artists for incorporation into installations.

The installation and virtual reality artists' studios

An almost paradoxical relationship exists between installation and virtual reality artists and their studios. Since installation is site-specific and virtual reality is computer-based, to some extent the 'studio' or creative realm of these artists is the public space or cyberspace where their work finds final expression. Installation covers a very broad range of work, and its creators incorporate diverse materials into their art. A digital installation artist's studio will therefore not be radically different from that of a traditional installation artist, aside from the addition of a computer and perhaps some computer-assisted manufacturing equipment and/or an electronics bench. Since the software and hardware used are quite elaborate, virtual reality art is generally a collaborative project between artist and programmer and often involves a larger creative team. Presently, virtual reality hardware and software still remain at the very high end of computing. However, the gap between virtual reality systems and personal computers has begun to narrow, making these technologies even more accessible to artists and their audiences. For example, in 2002, Char Davies ported two of her seminal works to the PC platform from a high-end computing environment.

The practitioners

The artists in this chapter represent a broad range of approaches to installation and virtual reality art. Char Davies, a pioneer of this art form, describes her immersive virtual reality environments Osmose (p. 29) and Ephémère (pp. 104–05) as works 'known for their embodying interface, painterly aesthetic and evocation of landscape'. Classics of their genre, they completely absorb the viewer in alternative worlds. Jeremy Gardiner also approaches virtual reality from a painterly perspective. In his Purbeck Light Years (pp. 108–09), the participant uses a video-game engine to navigate a three-dimensional landscape that incorporates the artist's paintings as well as the elements of time and weather. Mathieu Briand's work explores the virtual world through video headsets and transmitters. In SYS*05.ReE*03/SE*1\ MoE*2-4 (p. 102), viewers are able to 'see through each other's eyes' by the transmission of a video image from one person's headset to a small screen in the other participant's headset. Grahame Weinbren's installations invite us to explore and to rethink the world of cinema. The viewer is able to interact with the works, which offers a sense of partial authorship during the experience. While Erl King and Sonata are based on narrative, in Frames (p. 116) Weinbren invites the viewer to engage with the artwork's characters, who are based on Hugh Diamond's 19th-century photographs of psychiatric patients.

While virtual reality and digital cinema draw the participant into the content of the work, other installation artists use architectural elements and public space as the venue for their art. Shih-Chieh Huang constructs environments with various materials, including plastic sheeting, bottles and tubing, and then animates them through sensor-controlled fans, pumps and other electronic equipment (pp. 102, 113). Different lighting schemes are also used to add an other-worldly atmosphere. Erwin Redl uses large-scale light installations as architectural elements with which he constructs virtual reality spaces (what he calls 'reverse engineering'), thus creating the effect of a virtual space without the complex hardware and software interfaces normally required (pp. 119–21).

Other artists straddle the borders between print and installation. For example, Diane Fenster prints images on fabric and then creates an environment with these images in a gallery space (p. 106), while artists such as Ian Haig (p. 112) and Federico Muelas (p. 119) build installations in which multiple technologies are employed to engage the viewer.

Anticipating the future possibilities of installation art is exciting, as new technologies continue to emerge that will enable even greater control over these created environments. It is likely that wall-size LCD panels will soon be available to artists, as well as other technologies that we have not yet imagined. Irrespective of individual concepts, approaches or techniques, installation and virtual reality are vibrant forms of contemporary art. The digital perspective has brought artists who work in these areas powerful tools and new sources of creative expression.

REALITY IS ONLY A CONVENTION THAT ALMOST NEVER COINCIDES WITH WHAT IS TANGIBLE AROUND US. A LARGE PART OF WHAT WE CONSIDER REALITY, INCLUDING THOSE CLOSEST AND NEAREST TO US, IS NOTHING BUT THE PRODUCT OF SELF-DECEIT ... THE WORD 'REALITY' IS NO MORE THAN A PANACEA, A GREAT PANDORA'S BOX.

JOSÉ CARLOS CASADO

Below left

MATHIEU BRIAND, *SYS*05.ReE*03/ SE*1\MoE*2-4*, 2004. INSTALLATION VIEW FROM 'DERRIÈRE LE MONDE FLOTTANT', 2004

This piece challenges our notions of perception, location and visual language. Participants wear video headsets surmounted with cameras that allow them to switch between the views of the other participants. Virtual connections are created between the participants by the sharing of each other's viewpoints. The result is what the artist calls 'controlled schizophrenia'.

Below right

BRODY CONDON AND SHIH-CHIEH HUANG, *DERESFX.KILL (KARMAPHYSICS.5.0AMP)*, 2003. CUSTOM ELECTRONICS, FOUND OBJECTS, GAME MODIFICATION (UNREAL 2003), 244 X 122 X 122 CM (8 X 4 X 4 FT)

This installation is a collaboration between Shih-Chieh Huang and Brody Condon, and consists of custom lighting, electronics and a modified computer game based on Unreal 2003. Playful viewer interaction causes the appropriate game characters to shake violently in space.

Opposite

JOSÉ CARLOS CASADO AND HARKAITZ CANO, *PANDORA'S BOX (REVISITED).v03*, 2001. INTERACTIVE VIDEO INSTALLATION

José Carlos Casado and Harkaitz Cano combine live action with computer animation to express their creative vision. *Pandora's Box (revisited).v03* exists in several forms, including a digital video, an installation and as digital prints. The artists used a plethora of techniques to produce the work, including complex compositing of images and 3D animation. They explore the issues of personal identity and the interaction of human beings with alternate worlds and realities, asking viewers to question their sense of identity and self.

MY GOAL IS TO USE IMMERSIVE VIRTUAL SPACE TO COLLAPSE THE BOUNDARIES BETWEEN SUBJECT AND OBJECT, INTERIOR AND EXTERIOR, AND SELF AND OTHER. IN DOING SO, MY INTENT IS TO REFRESH OUR PERCEPTION OF BEING IN THE WORLD. I WANT TO RESENSITIZE PARTICIPANTS TO THE EXTRAORDINARINESS OF BEING ALIVE, SENTIENT AND EMBODIED, HERE NOW AMONG ALL THIS, IMMERSED AS WE ARE SO BRIEFLY IN THE FLOW OF LIFE THROUGH SPACE AND TIME.
CHAR DAVIES

Opposite
**CHAR DAVIES, *SEEDS*, 1998. DIGITAL STILL
IMAGE CAPTURED DURING IMMERSIVE
PERFORMANCE OF THE VIRTUAL ENVIRONMENT
*EPHÉMÈRE***

Ephémère is experienced by wearing a stereoscopic
head-mounted display and a motion-tracking vest to
record the participants's breath and balance, enabling
him or her to float through its virtual realms. It is spatially
structured along 3 vertical levels: landscape, under-earth
and interior body, and also uses gaze to interact, causing
elements to respond to the visitor. Each exploration is
unique: *Ephémère*'s sounds and visual elements are
engaged in constant transformation. They all come into
being, linger and pass away in keeping with *Ephémère*'s
emphasis on mortality and the ephemerality of life.

Below
**CHAR DAVIES, *FOREST STREAM*, 1998. DIGITAL
STILL IMAGE CAPTURED DURING IMMERSIVE
PERFORMANCE OF THE VIRTUAL ENVIRONMENT
*EPHÉMÈRE***

When exhibited as an installation, *Ephémère* consists
not only of a private chamber for immersion, but also
a screen whereby the silhouette of the participant's body
can be seen by an audience. This installation design is
intended to highlight the significant role that embodiment
plays in the subjective experience of virtual space.

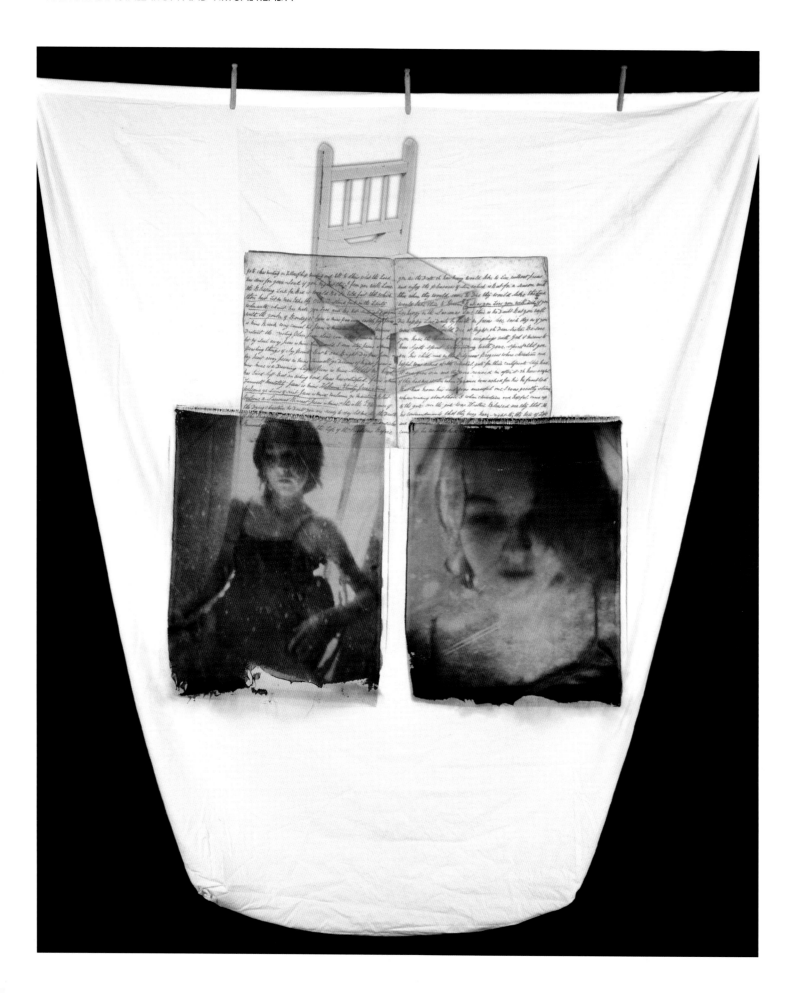

MY WORK EMBODIES THE HIDDEN POETRY OF THE ORDINARY, MAKING VISIBLE WHAT PREVIOUSLY WAS HIDDEN. *THE SECRETS OF THE MAGDALEN LAUNDRIES* EXPLORES THE THEME OF IMAGINATION IN THE INNER LIFE. DREAMING, REVERIE AND FANTASY ARE WAYS OF BEING THAT MAKE THE REALITY OF CIRCUMSTANCE MORE TOLERABLE.
DIANE FENSTER

Opposite
DIANE FENSTER, *THE SECRETS OF THE MAGDALEN LAUNDRIES* (DETAIL), 2000. PHOTO INSTALLATION, DYE-SUBLIMATION DIGITAL PRINTS AND 20 X 24 INCH POLAROID IMAGES TRANSFERRED ONTO BEDSHEETS

This installation, of which images form a primary component, creates a metaphoric laundry environment that documents Irish women who were incarcerated in laundry prisons. Consisting of fifteen bed sheets that hang into antique washtubs, the imagery proposes the idea that a retreat into inner fantasy was one of the ways in which the women survived their ordeal. The gallery is also permeated with sound recordings of women speaking and whispering in Gaelic.

Right
MASAKI FUJIHATA, *BEYOND PAGES*, 1995–99. MULTI-MEDIA INSTALLATION, 4 X 5 M (13 X 16½ FT)

Beyond Pages takes the participant on an exploration that causes him or her to rethink the nature of the book. Upon sitting down at a desk, one sees a leather-bound volume projected onto a screen and a light pen masquerading as a pencil. By moving through the pages, the participant is taken on a wonderful journey: 3D elements move across the surface of the 'paper', their movement coupled with acoustic signals, lights switch on and video doors open. In this work Masaki Fujihata calls into question the idea of the book as an interface.

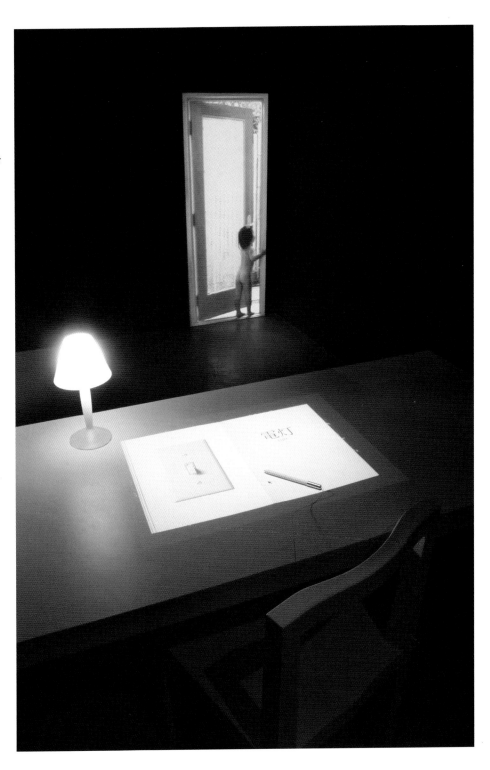

PURBECK LIGHT YEARS IS A MIXTURE OF OLD AND NEW – HYBRID TECHNIQUES THAT COMBINE CHARACTERISTICS OF COMPUTER ANIMATION , PAINTING AND DRAWING AND IMMERSIVE VIRTUAL REALITY. INSIDE THIS VIRTUAL SPACE IS A WHOLE WORLD REIMAGINED, A TOPOGRAPHICAL LANDSCAPE OF CORFE CASTLE MODELLED IN THREE DIMENSIONS, SILENT AND SECRET, A PLACE OF ACCUMULATED HISTORY. THE GRAPHICS HELP CAPTURE THE IMAGINATION BY CREATING A SUBTLE AND AMBIGUOUS WORLD WHERE THE ATMOSPHERE IS LUMINOUS AND THE SPACE THREE-DIMENSIONAL. THE COLOUR WE SEE REPRESENTS SCATTERING, REFRACTION AND DIFFRACTION OF SUNLIGHT BY PARTICLES IN THE ATMOSPHERE. WEATHER SYSTEMS COME AND GO, NIGHT FOLLOWS DAY AND SEASONS CHANGE IN REAL TIME.
JEREMY GARDINER

Opposite and above
**JEREMY GARDINER, *SPRING* AND *WINTER* –
PURBECK LIGHT YEARS, 2003. DIGITAL
FRAME CAPTURED FROM 3D INTERACTIVE
VIRTUAL ENVIRONMENT**
Left
**JEREMY GARDINER, *PURBECK LIGHT YEARS*,
2003. IMMERSIVE VIRTUAL ENVIRONMENT
WITH LARGE-SCALE INTERACTIVE
PROJECTIONS**
This interactive installation blends traditional painting
and digital media. The original paintings used as
inspiration for the work are on one wall, while viewers
interact with the virtual reality piece on another.
Jeremy Gardiner collaborated with programmer
Anthony Head to create this work, which is controlled
by video game hardware and software. In 2003,
Purbeck Light Years was the first digital work to win the
Peterborough Prize.

VICTORIA VESNA, *NANO*, 2004. LARGE-SCALE INTERACTIVE PROJECT, NINE INTERCONNECTED INSTALLATIONS

Victoria Vesna's recent work includes *Nano*, a series of installations that present the world of nanoscience through a participatory aesthetic experience. In the central area of the exhibition is the large Inner Cell, where participants interact with molecular forms. Using just their shadows, they are able to manipulate large-scale projected images of carbon molecules.

HEXAGONS ARE FOUND IN MANY STRUCTURES IN NATURE, INCLUDING BEEHIVES AND THE RECENTLY DISCOVERED BUCKYBALLS AND BUCKYTUBES, THE PRIMARY MOLECULES DRIVING NANOTECHNOLOGY. MY GOAL IS TO MAKE FAR-REACHING CONNECTIONS BETWEEN THE SOCIAL STRUCTURES WE UNCONSCIOUSLY BUILD AND THE ONES THAT ARE INHERENTLY THE BUILDING BLOCKS OF NATURE.
VICTORIA VESNA

Left
IAN HAIG, *WEB DEVOLUTION*, 1998. MIXED-MEDIA, 100 X 220 X 84 CM (39¼ X 86⅝ X 33 IN)
Ian Haig uses humour and satire to explore our sometimes perverse relationship with technology. *Web Devolution* takes the form of an intricate sculpture connected to the internet and provides a witty take on the roles that machine culture plays in our lives.

Opposite
SHIH-CHIEH HUANG, *RTI-#2*, 2003. PLASTIC CONTAINER, MICROCONTROLLER, 61 X 30.5 X 76.2 CM (24 X 12 X 30 IN)
Shih-Chieh Huang's unique environmental pieces – composed of ordinary materials such as clear plastic sheeting, plastic ties, fluorescent lights, water and tubing – are brought to life through the use of sensors, switches and robotic devices. Huang's site-specific, immersive installations lead the viewer through a fantastic maze of colour, motion and sound.

THE ABILITY TO CHANGE THE SENTENCE IS A SYMBOLIC GESTURE: IT IMPLIES THAT WE DO NOT ACCEPT ITS MEANING IN THE FORM WE INHERITED IT, AND THAT NEW MEANINGS EMERGE AS WE SEEK TO CHANGE IT.
EDUARDO KAC

Above
EDUARDO KAC, *GENESIS*, 1999.
TRANSGENIC NET INSTALLATION

Eduardo Kac translated a sentence from the *Book of Genesis* into Morse code and then converted it into DNA base pairs using a process developed specifically for this work. The sentence reads: 'Let man have dominion over the fish of the sea, and over the fowl of the air, and over every living thing that moves upon the earth.' It was chosen for what it implies about the notion of humanity's divinely sanctioned supremacy over nature. Kac incorporated the synthetic *Genesis* gene into bacteria, which were shown in the gallery. Web participants could turn on an ultraviolet light remotely, which caused real, biological mutations in the bacteria and changed its 'biblical sentence'. *Genesis* explores the relationships between ethics, biology, belief systems and information technology.

Opposite
EDUARDO KAC, *MOVE 36*, 2002–04.
TRANSGENIC INSTALLATION WITH DIGITAL VIDEO

This installation invites the viewer to ponder the limits of the human mind and the increasing capabilities of computers and robots. The work references the dramatic chess move made by the computer Deep Blue against world champion Gary Kasparov in 1997, a competition that could be characterized as a match between the greatest chess player who ever lived and the greatest chess player who never lived.

MOVE 36 PRESENTS A CHESSBOARD MADE OF EARTH (DARK SQUARES) AND WHITE SAND (LIGHT SQUARES) IN THE MIDDLE OF THE ROOM. POSITIONED EXACTLY WHERE DEEP BLUE MADE ITS *MOVE 36* IS A PLANT WHOSE GENOME INCORPORATES A NEW GENE THAT I CREATED SPECIFICALLY FOR THIS WORK. THE GENE USES ASCII (THE UNIVERSAL COMPUTER CODE FOR REPRESENTING BINARY NUMBERS AS ROMAN CHARACTERS) TO TRANSLATE TO THE FOUR BASES OF GENETICS.
EDUARDO KAC

FRAMES **ALLOWS THE USER TO AFFECT THE STORY BY POINTING AT THE SCREEN AND THUS TRANSFORMING AN ACTRESS INTO A 19TH-CENTURY MADWOMAN. THIS TRANSFORMATION IS THE TIMELINE OF THE PIECE, WHILE THE NARRATIVE IS IN THE COMPLEXITIES OF THE RELATIONSHIP OF PHOTOGRAPHER TO SUBJECT, AND PHOTOGRAPHER TO VIEWER. THIS IS A HIGHLY NON-LINEAR NARRATIVE STRUCTURE, AND ONE THAT CAN ONLY BE FULLY EXPRESSED IN A NON-LINEAR MEDIUM.**
GRAHAME WEINBREN

Opposite
**GRAHAME WEINBREN,
FRAMES, 1999. 3-CHANNEL,
2-USER INTERACTIVE CINEMA
INSTALLATION, COMPUTER,
LASER-DISC PLAYERS,
PERIPHERAL EQUIPMENT,
VARIABLE DIMENSIONS**
Empty frames are suspended in
front of projected photographs of
mental patients taken in the 1800s
and a video of actors dressed
as patients. As the viewer points
through the frame, an interaction
is triggered between the images
and the video, the actor being
transformed into a patient.

Below right
**NOAH WARDRIP-FRUIN,
SASCHA BECKER, JOSH
CARROLL, ROBERT COOVER,
ANDREW MCCLAIN AND
SHAWN GREENLEE, *SCREEN*,
2003–05. VIRTUAL REALITY
CAVE, BODY TRACKING,
APPROX. 2.4 X 2.4 X 2.4 M
(8 X 8 X 8 FT)**
In this work, the viewer is
surrounded by a plethora of
words, text, type fragments and
spatialized sound. This flow of
text is intended to create a type
of stream-of-consciousness, as
different associations are ignited
by the visuals.

**SCREEN BEGINS AS A READING AND LISTENING EXPERIENCE.
IT COMBINES FAMILIAR GAME MECHANICS WITH VIRTUAL
REALITY TECHNOLOGY TO CREATE AN EXPERIENCE OF BODILY
INTERACTION WITH TEXT. MEMORY TEXTS APPEAR ON THE
WALLS, SURROUNDING THE READER. THEN WORDS BEGIN
TO COME LOOSE. THE READER FINDS HE OR SHE CAN KNOCK
THEM BACK WITH A HAND, AND THE EXPERIENCE BECOMES
A KIND OF PLAY. AT THE SAME TIME, THE LANGUAGE OF THE
TEXT, TOGETHER WITH THE UNCANNY EXPERIENCE OF
TOUCHING WORDS, CREATES AN EXPERIENCE THAT DOESN'T
SETTLE EASILY INTO THE USUAL WAYS OF THINKING ABOUT
GAMEPLAY OR VIRTUAL REALITY. WORDS PEEL FASTER AND
FASTER, STRUCK WORDS DON'T ALWAYS RETURN TO WHERE
THEY CAME FROM, AND WORDS WITH NOWHERE TO GO CAN
BREAK APART. EVENTUALLY, WHEN TOO MANY ARE OFF THE
WALL, THE REST PEEL LOOSE, SWIRL AROUND THE READER,
AND COLLAPSE.
NOAH WARDRIP-FRUIN**

DAVID ROKEBY, *GIVER OF NAMES*, 1991 – PRESENT. INTERACTIVE DIGITAL INSTALLATION, CUSTOM SOFTWARE
Canadian artist David Rokeby uses machine intelligence to explore issues of human communication and the structure of language. *Giver of Names* is a computer system that gives objects names. Visitors choose one or more objects and place them on a pedestal, which is surveyed by a camera. The computer grabs an image of the object or objects and processes the graphic information on many levels (analysis of outline, texture and colour, division into separate parts), all of which are visible to viewers on a small projection above the pedestal. The computer's attempts to make sense, through association, of what it sees lead to increasingly abstract conclusions, which it then voices aloud in English. New forms of meaning and connections are thus revealed.

Left
FEDERICO MUELAS, *DRIPPING SOUNDS*, 2002. AUDIOVISUAL INSTALLATION, STEEL, GLASS, ACRYLIC, ALUMINIUM AND ELECTRONIC COMPONENTS, 4.3 X 3.4 M (14 X 11¼ FT)
Dripping Sounds is an audiovisual installation in which the movement of drops of ink expanding into clear water determines the type of sounds that fill the installation space. In his creative work Federico Muelas aims to reveal the natural order that underlies what is often perceived as chaos

Below
ERWIN REDL, *MATRIX IV*, 2001. LED INSTALLATION, BROOKLYN BRIDGE ANCHORAGE, NEW YORK, 15 X 15 X 6 M (50 X 50 X 20 FT).

Overleaf
ERWIN REDL, *MATRIX II*, 2000–03. LED LIGHT INSTALLATION, RIVA GALLERY, NEW YORK, VARIABLE DIMENSIONS
Erwin Redl's large-scale, site-specific installations make use of digital technology in a unique fashion. His works consist of curtains of small, bright LED lights hanging in complete darkness that seem to convert the planes and grids of virtual space into a physical environment that can be experienced directly by users.

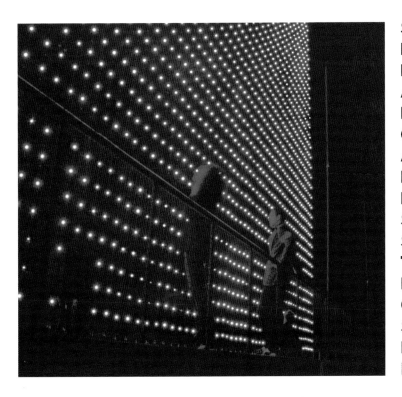

SINCE 1997, I HAVE INVESTIGATED THE PROCESS OF 'REVERSE ENGINEERING' BY (RE)TRANSLATING THE ABSTRACT AESTHETIC LANGUAGE OF VIRTUAL REALITY AND THREE-DIMENSIONAL COMPUTER MODELLING BACK INTO AN ARCHITECTURAL ENVIRONMENT BY MEANS OF LARGE-SCALE LIGHT INSTALLATIONS. IN THIS BODY OF WORK, SPACE IS EXPERIENCED AS A SECOND SOCIAL SKIN, WHICH IS TRANSFORMED THROUGH MY ARCHITECTURAL INTERVENTION. DUE TO THE VERY NATURE OF ARCHITECTURE, PARTICIPATING BY SIMPLY BEING 'PRESENT' IS AN INTEGRAL PART OF THE INSTALLATIONS.
ERWIN REDL

PERFORMANCE, MUSIC AND SOUND ART

While installation art and virtual reality refer primarily to artistic environments, it is the individual artist who is at the centre of performance, music and sound art. What we now call performance art emerged from the early 20th-century movements of Futurism, Dada and Surrealism, whose members often hosted provocative events that prompted audiences to reconsider their ideas about art. Among the many Futurist manifestos that were adapted for stage performance was Luigi Russolo's *Art of Noises*, which asserted that machine sounds were a viable form of music. The Dadaists and Surrealists experimented with different forms of performance and sound art. Oskar Schlemmer, who served for a period as head of the theatre workshop at the Bauhaus, was instrumental in transforming the stage into a three-dimensional art space, thus integrating the principle of unifying the arts using performance as the primary medium.

In America, John Cage and Merce Cunningham, a composer and choreographer respectively, were very influential figures in the world of avant-garde music performance, sound art and dance, and frequent collaborators. Cage approached environmental sound as the building blocks of music composition and likened his 'sound library' to a musical instrument. Cunningham sought new experimental approaches to dance and performance. Throughout the 1950s and 1960s, similar artistic sensibilities found their expression in gallery events and happenings, trends that led to the establishment of Experiments in Art and Technology (EAT) in

1966. Founded by engineers Billy Klüver and Fred Waldhauer and artists Robert Rauschenberg and Robert Whitman, EAT was a benchmark for encouraging collaboration among artists and scientists, and eventually became an international organization that included thousands of members. Composer Pauline Oliveros began developing a system in the mid-1960s called the Expanded Instrument System (EIS), which allows for improvizing musicians to collaborate through the use of tape loops and foot pedals, later adding digital processing devices. Oliveros's approach to music performance is based on the concept of deep listening – a more spiritual, meditative approach to experiencing music and sound art. The Fluxus artists' collective, which flourished during the 1960s and 1970s, was an international avant-garde group that championed artistic experimentation combined with social and political activism. The group included such artists as Joseph Beuys, John Cage, Charlotte Moorman, Yoko Ono and Nam June Paik, and many incorporated technology, performance, music and sound art into their work.

One important technological development that revolutionized electronic music was the synthesizer, invented by Robert Moog in 1964. Twenty years later, several synthesizer manufacturers banded together and adopted MIDI, the Musical Instrument Digital Interface, which enabled electronic instruments from different manufacturers to communicate with each other. MIDI has the ability to record the nuances of a performance through digital data rather than audio files, registering pitch, note on, note off, velocity and aftertouch. Since this data is available in a form that can easily be edited, copied and manipulated, a musician can correct mistakes, add harmony parts, change the voice of the instrument, or integrate any number of other features that expand the composer's palette. Recently, software emulation of synthesizers and inexpensive hardware have brought sophisticated sound modelling to the computer, particularly laptops, which are widely used for live performance by audio and video DJs.

Music and sound continue to play a significant role in the contemporary art world. In their search to stimulate and influence the audience/participant, artists produce immersive environments that skilfully combine audio and visual elements, as well as internet-based projects that encourage user interaction to shape sound worlds and artworks that feature sound and nothing else. From a practical point of view, advances in technology have allowed artists access to music and sound production environments; performance systems; affordable, user-friendly equipment; and off-the-shelf software, all of which have greatly increased their creative options. Once a work has been completed, technology also ensures artists wide distribution in such forms as CDs, DVDs, MP3 files and the numerous ways in which audio and video content can be streamed over the internet.

The phrase 'audio precedes video' aptly describes the sequence in which technological advances in analogue and digital equipment occurred. For example, the ability to record audio material onto tape preceded the invention of videotape. Since the computing power needed to handle audio data is considerably less than that required by video, the conversion of audio production to an all-digital environment occurred relatively quickly, and although some recording studios still use analogue equipment, the vast majority have converted to digital methods of production. In 1980 the Compact Disk (CD) 'Red Book' standard was established. It is based on a sample rate of 44.1 kHz and a bit depth of 16 – the level at which the human ear does not detect any digital artifacts. While current recording systems have gone far beyond this standard, it did mark the point at which this technology matured.

The invention of the MP3 format was a further milestone in the audio revolution. This data compression system, famous for its ability to produce digital music files that can be easily downloaded, was very quickly adopted by networked communities, independent sounds artists and musicians for the purposes of file sharing and data exchange. The Apple iPod and its Podcasts are examples of commercial technology that offer distribution of music and sound art. Multi-channel sound is an emerging trend in music, performance and sound art. Fifty years ago audio recording moved from single-channel, monophonic sound to stereo. Now that DVD is one of the fastest-growing consumer technologies, interest in surround-sound and multi-channel sound art has increased. DVD-Audio technology brings studio-quality sound not only to home entertainment systems, but also to galleries and museums.

The practical application of digital sound in performance, music and sound art
The creative technologies available to performance, music and sound artists have changed dramatically in the past few decades. Whereas multi-track recording previously required very specialized, costly equipment, current software is relatively easy to use, affordable, and can run on most personal computers. The primary component of a professional digital music recording system is a computer with software such as Digidesign Pro Tools, which offers high-quality, multi-channel recording, as well as MIDI options and integration with video. In order to benefit from multiple channels of input and output, higher-level systems use an additional audio card and external hardware. A wide variety of software plug-ins for added capabilities and sound processing effects is also available. Other popular software applications include Symbolic Sound Corporation's Kyma X, Propellerhead Software Reason, Steinberg Cubase and Apple Logic Pro.

Increasingly, performance artists are incorporating sensors and other devices into their repertoire. These tools enable the control of different machines and media during a performance in a sophisticated fashion, such as sensors worn on the body of the performer that control sound and visuals. Different locations on the stage can be designated so that floor tiles, for instance, trigger changes in lighting or video sequences. This technology, such as the I-CubeX MIDI interface, allows the environment to be responsive or permits the performer to control the responses – in some cases both. Other artists configure their interface and sensors through software environments such as Cycling '74 Max/MSP. DJs prefer to work with laptop computers that function as live performance systems with audio and video programmes that they can manipulate real-time. Today's digital artists and musicians have indeed benefited from advances in technology, and more importantly are making invaluable contributions to the evolution of digital and contemporary art.

The practitioners
The artists mentioned here come from a broad spectrum of backgrounds. While some have entered via careers in music and art, others started by writing their own custom software. The works that follow reflect different aspects of these disciplines: software-mediated performance, multi-media theatre and performance, visual music, networked performance and collaborative sound art. David Rokeby's *Very Nervous System* (p. 126) is a landmark piece in interactive music, for which he wrote custom software and configured specialized hardware. Stephen Vitiello (pp. 140–41) is a sound artist who bases his work on 'natural' sounds, both urban and rural. Ben Neill invented the 'mutantrumpet' (p. 128), an instrument that not only plays in the traditional way, but also sends MIDI instructions that modify the visual backdrop. Joan La Barbara (p. 133) and Golan Levin create collaborative, real-time performances with their art, and Levin came to work in this field though his background as a software artist (pp. 172–73). Beryl Korot and Steve Reich collaborated on *Three Tales* (p. 127) to create a work of multi-media musical theatre. Emerging artists Leesa and Nicole Abahuni, known as the 'Turbo Twins', bring robotic technology to performance through an interactive experience (p. 134).

The widespread availability of recording software has generated an increased interest among artists to create performance, music and sound artworks. The diversity of venues that now support these artistic genres – from museums, galleries, nightclubs and theatres to distribution via the internet – offers a multitude of choices to audiences.

I CREATED *VERY NERVOUS SYSTEM* FOR MANY REASONS, BUT PERHAPS THE MOST PERVASIVE REASON WAS A SIMPLE IMPULSE TOWARDS CONTRARINESS. THE INTERFACE IS UNUSUAL BECAUSE IT IS INVISIBLE AND VERY DIFFUSE, OCCUPYING A LARGE VOLUME OF SPACE, WHEREAS MOST INTERFACES ARE FOCUSED AND DEFINITE. THE INTERFACE BECOMES A ZONE OF EXPERIENCE, OF MULTI-DIMENSIONAL ENCOUNTER. THE LANGUAGE OF ENCOUNTER IS INITIALLY UNCLEAR, BUT EVOLVES AS ONE EXPLORES AND EXPERIENCES. THE INSTALLATION COULD BE DESCRIBED AS A SORT OF INSTRUMENT THAT YOU PLAY WITH YOUR BODY, BUT THAT IMPLIES A LEVEL OF CONTROL THAT I AM NOT PARTICULARLY INTERESTED IN. I AM INTERESTED IN CREATING A COMPLEX AND RESONANT RELATIONSHIP BETWEEN THE INTERACTOR AND THE SYSTEM.
DAVID ROKEBY

Opposite
DAVID ROKEBY, *VERY NERVOUS SYSTEM*, 1986–91. COMPUTER, SYNTHESIZER, CAMERA, CUSTOM SOFTWARE, AMPLIFIER AND SPEAKERS, VARIABLE DIMENSIONS

Very Nervous System relied on subtle movements of the body to create sounds and music. Its innovative interface, which linked video, motion-tracking software, music and movement, made it a benchmark work of interactive art and is still used by composers, choreographers, musicians and artists.

Below
BERYL KOROT AND STEVE REICH, *ACT 1: HINDENBURG* AND *ACT 2: BIKINI*, FROM *THREE TALES*, 2002. DOCUMENTARY DIGITAL VIDEO OPERA

*Three Tale*s is a work of music theatre that uses events from the last century to explore the implications of developing technology. *Act 1: Hindenburg* recounts the story of the infamous zeppelin, while *Act 2: Bikini* focuses on the atomic bomb testing undertaken at the Bikini atoll and the relocation of its people. *Act 3: Dolly* (not shown) comments on the 1997 cloning of an adult sheep in Scotland, as well as on robots and cyborgs. In addition to musicians and singers, the theatrical setting includes video projections of a digitally created mélange of film and video footage, photographic stills and text. Beryl Korot, a pioneer in multi-channel video art, approached the project as a way of bringing video art into a theatrical context. Steve Reich is one of the most respected contemporary composers, and innovations in composition, rhythm, orchestration and the use of speech and sound manipulation are part of his ever-evolving creative repertoire.

I BEGAN WORKING WITH COMPUTERS AS COMPOSITIONAL AND PERFORMANCE TOOLS IN THE LATE 1980s AND HAVE BEEN IMMERSED IN THE DIGITAL ARTS EVER SINCE. IN ADDITION TO THE EXCITEMENT OF WORKING IN SUCH A RAPIDLY-EVOLVING FORM, DIGITAL ART IS MAKING AN IMPORTANT AESTHETIC CONTRIBUTION THROUGH ITS BREAKING DOWN OF MANY PREVIOUSLY IMPENETRABLE BARRIERS BETWEEN GENRES, DISCIPLINES, ETC. THE EVOLUTION OF NEW INTERACTIVE DIGITAL VIDEO TECHNOLOGIES HAS MADE IT POSSIBLE FOR MY IDEA OF INTEGRATING SOUND AND VISION TO BE REALIZED ON A MUCH MORE ADVANCED LEVEL.
BEN NEILL

BEN NEILL, *MUTANTRUMPET*, 1990. INTERACTIVE CONTROLLER
Mutantrumpet is a composite electro-acoustic instrument. Initially created in 1984, the original subsequently underwent several variations. Based on a traditional trumpet and enhanced with MIDI and video controls, the *Mutantrumpet* represents a new hybrid instrument for performance.

BEN NEILL AND BILL JONES, *AUTOMOTIVE TOUR*, 2002. MUTANTRUMPET, MIDI-CONTROLLED VIDEO PERFORMANCE
This live performance at the House of Blues in Chicago featured composer and performer Ben Neill on his *Mutantrumpet* and Bill Jones controlling a digital video backdrop. The choice of music – 21st-century jazz – matches the improvizational nature of the audiovisual performance. The video for *Automotive* was created from remixed advertisements for Volkswagen cars, for which Neill had composed the music.

Left
CARSTEN NICOLAI, PERFORMANCE IN MONTREAL, 2001
In addition to presenting his work in galleries and museums, Carsten Nicolai also performs his electronic music and sound on stage, both as a solo artist and collaboratively.

Below
CARSTEN NICOLAI IN COLLABORATION WITH MARKO PELIJHAN, *POLAR*, 2000. INTERACTIVE MULTI-MEDIA INSTALLATION
Paired participants enter the installation with a 'POL' interface device (developed for this project) and collect data (images, sounds and temperature readings) for a set amount of time. The information from the POL is then analysed and converted into keywords that appear on monitors. A keyword is selected and a specially developed search system collects information from various databases and websites on the internet.

TO DEFINE A COMPLEX SYSTEM THAT GENERATES SOUNDS OR IMAGES, AND THEN MODULATE IT ... COMBINE IT WITH OTHER ELEMENTS OR USE IT AS A NEW STARTING POINT.... THE COMPUTER IS A PERFECT PARTNER: IT IS TIRELESS, SURPRISING, FLEXIBLE.
JUAN ANTONIO LLEÓ

Opposite
JUAN ANTONIO LLEÓ, *TORRE DE ESPEJOS (TOWER OF MIRRORS)*, 2003. INTERACTIVE INSTALLATION, VARIABLE DIMENSIONS
Juan Antonio Lleó's installation combines sculpture, video and music. Developed in collaboration with Antonio Alvarado, *Torre de Espejos* is composed of everyday objects, including a dozen plastic mirrors, which are illuminated by a video projector and several spotlights. Upon entering the installation, the viewer/participant finds his or her response to the music projected onto a screen and combined with video footage of a virtual reality environment.

Below
JUAN ANTONIO LLEÓ, *MIDIVERSO*, 1994–2002. INTERACTIVE INSTALLATION, VARIABLE DIMENSIONS
Designed to be experienced by large groups of people, this work consists of a large Plexiglas hemisphere equipped with thirty-two velocity-sensitive MIDI buttons. Each button triggers a different noise, and viewers can influence the sound by pressing the buttons at different speeds.

THE INTRODUCTION OF A NEW MEDIUM INVARIABLY CHANGES HOW ART HAS BEEN EVALUATED. WE ARE DOING JUST THAT RIGHT NOW. EVENTUALLY, THE ELEMENTS WE HAVE ADDED TO THE CONVERSATION BECOME THE 'TRADITIONAL CRITERIA', AND THEN A NEW MEDIUM COMES ALONG THAT ADDS TO THE CONVERSATION. IT ALWAYS TAKES TIME FOR THE NEW TO BE A PART OF THE OLD. I'M JUST THRILLED TO BE AROUND AND WORKING NOW, AND NOT FIFTY YEARS FROM NOW, SO I'M PART OF THE EARLY CONVERSATION.
JOHN KLIMA

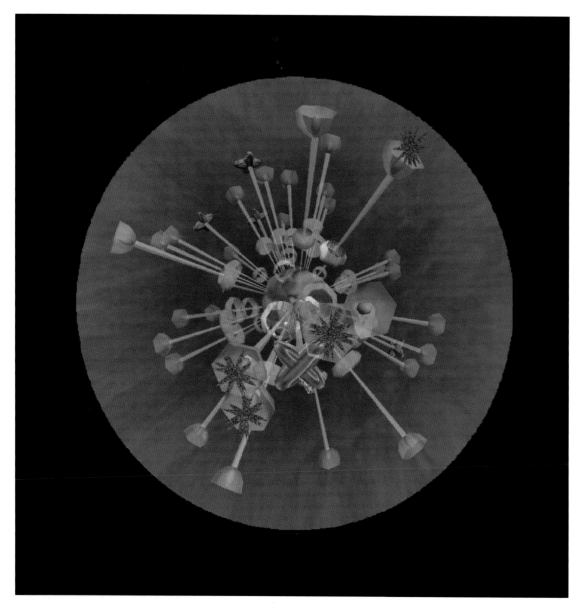

JOHN KLIMA, *GLASBEAD*, 1999. SOFTWARE
Glasbead has a multi-user musical interface and can exist as an installation or as net art. Users assign sounds to the 'flower' parts of the spherical, bouquet-like structure. The interactivity involves spinning the entire structure with a 'click and drag' motion or individually moving the elements of the interface to strike the 'flowers' and trigger various sounds. *Glasbead* can be played by as many as twenty online participants simultaneously, enabling them to share in the creation of complex soundscapes. John Klima named the project after Hermann Hesse's novel *The Glass Bead Game*, which describes a symbolic system in which art, music, sculpture, literature and other creative art forms are deconstructed into different combinations of glass beads.

Above left
JOAN LA BARBARA WITH GOLAN LEVIN, ZACH LIEBERMAN AND JAAP BLONK, *MESSA DI VOCE*, 2003. PERFORMANCE AT ARS ELECTRONICA, LINZ, AUSTRIA

Above right
JOAN LA BARBARA WITH GOLAN LEVIN, ZACH LIEBERMAN AND JAAP BLONK, *MESSA DI VOCE*, 2003. PERFORMANCE AT THE ULTRASOUND FESTIVAL, HUDDERSFIELD, ENGLAND

Joan La Barbara is a composer, performer and sound artist who explores the possibilities of the human voice in a series of ground-breaking works for voices, instruments and interactive technology. Her unique vocabulary of vocal techniques includes circular singing, ululation and glottal clicks.

***MESSA DI VOCE* IS CONCERNED WITH THE POETIC IMPLICATIONS OF MAKING THE HUMAN VOICE VISIBLE. THE CORE TECHNOLOGY THAT MAKES THIS POSSIBLE IS A CUSTOM SOFTWARE SYSTEM THAT INTEGRATES REAL-TIME COMPUTER VISION AND SPEECH ANALYSIS ALGORITHMS. A COMPUTER USES A VIDEO CAMERA TO TRACK THE LOCATIONS OF THE PERFORMERS' HEADS AND ANALYSES THE AUDIO SIGNALS COMING FROM THEIR MICROPHONES. IN RESPONSE, THE COMPUTER DISPLAYS VARIOUS KINDS OF VISUALIZATIONS ON A SCREEN BEHIND THE PERFORMERS. IN SOME OF THE VISUALIZATIONS, GRAPHIC ELEMENTS REPRESENT VOCAL SOUNDS AND ALSO SERVE AS A PLAYABLE INTERACTIVE INTERFACE BY WHICH PERFORMERS CAN RETRIGGER AND MANIPULATE THE SOUNDS.**
JOAN LA BARBARA, GOLAN LEVIN, ZACH LIEBERMAN AND JAAP BLONK

THE INVESTIGATION OF HOW THE SENSES ARE PERCEIVED AND THE EXPLORATION OF THE INTERRELATIONSHIPS BETWEEN THE VISUAL, AURAL AND THE TACTILE ARE THE ESSENCE OF OUR CURIOSITY. WE ARE COMMITTED TO EXAMINING POTENTIAL NETWORKS AND CREATING NEW FORMS OF PERCEPTION. ULTIMATELY, WE WISH OUR WORK TO CREATE NEW RELATIONSHIPS IN THE TERRITORY BETWEEN EXISTING AND NEW SENSORY SYSTEMS. THE ACTIVE FORGING OF TACTILE, AURAL AND VISUAL PERCEPTION BETWEEN HUMANS, AND IN COLLABORATION WITH TECHNOLOGY, ASKS QUESTIONS WHICH CAN YIELD WAYS OF BETTER UNDERSTANDING, SEEING AND HEARING NATURAL ORDER.
LEESA AND NICOLE ABAHUNI

LEESA AND NICOLE ABAHUNI, *CAPACITANCE*, 2003. PERFORMANCE AND INTERACTIVE INSTALLATION. INFRARED ROBOT, MARKER PENS, PLEXIGLAS, VINYL, CUSTOM CIRCUITRY, SPEAKERS, 182.9 X 121.9 X 182.9 CM (6 X 4 X 6 FT)
The 'performer' in this work was in fact a robot that received instructions on what to draw from participants' physical interactions with low-voltage circuits. The goal of *Capacitance* was to foster potential connections between human and machine.

LEESA AND NICOLE ABAHUNI, *CHAOTIC ROBOTIC SYNESTHESIA*, 2000. PERFORMANCE. 2 INFRARED ROBOTS, MICROCONTROLLED STAGE, COLOURED LIGHTS, 4 X 4 M (13 X 13 FT)
This performance, which was inspired by the theories of psychologist Jean Dauven, explored the concept of synaesthesia – a neural condition in which the stimulation of one sense, such as hearing, produces an effect in another of the senses, such as sight, so that synaesthetes can 'see' music or 'hear' colours. Several participants – two animators, seven musicians and two robots – created and interacted with sound and coloured lights on a stage linked to microcontrollers.

**RAIN ANNE ASHFORD, *DUSTHARPS*, 2000.
INTERACTIVE ARTWORK**
This interactive musical artwork unfolds as viewers
move a mouse over the graphics, creating different
sounds and animations. Rain Anne Ashford
encourages new interpretations of the traditional
media of drawing, painting and sound.

**I'M TOTALLY DRIVEN TO CREATE THINGS. I ANNOUNCED TO MY PARENTS AGED
FOUR THAT I WAS GOING TO BE AN ARTIST. I'VE BEEN PLAYING WITH SOUND
AND VISUALS AS SEPARATE ELEMENTS EVER SINCE, ALTHOUGH MULTI-MEDIA
APPLICATIONS AVAILABLE FOR HOME COMPUTERS ENABLED ME TO FIND A WAY
OF BRINGING THESE DIFFERENT MEDIA TOGETHER, USING A PROCESS WHICH
I REALLY ENJOYED. I LOVE THE INTERNET, IT'S A GREAT MEDIUM/ENVIRONMENT
TO WORK WITH.**
RAIN ANNE ASHFORD

EACH OF THE IMAGES SHOWN HERE IS ONE OF THE 1000 OR SO THAT MIGHT UNFOLD DURING ONE MINUTE OF A MUSICAL PERFORMANCE. THEY ARE GENERATED IN REAL-TIME UNDER THE CONTROL OF A PLAYER WHO IS RESPONDING TO, AND INTERACTING WITH, THE MUSICIANS. MIDI CONTROLLERS AFFECT THE COLOUR, SHAPE, SIZE, PERSISTENCE AND OTHER CHARACTERISTICS OF SIMPLE OBJECTS SUCH AS LINES, ARCS AND POLYGONS.

FRED COLLOPY

FRED COLLOPY, *PHISPIRALS* AND *WOOD & WATER*, 2004. IMAGE CAPTURES OF LIVE PERFORMANCES

Fred Collopy, a programming pioneer, develops digital software that allows visual artists to play with animated graphic images in the same way that musicians play with sounds. The first version of his Imager software was devised on the Apple II computer in 1977. His creative work investigates visual music – the unification of musical and visual elements into an integrated sensory experience.

ATAU TANAKA AND KASPER TOEPLITZ, *GLOBAL STRING*, 2000. INTERACTIVE MUSIC INSTALLATION

Global String is a networked music installation which is comprised of two sites, each with a steel cable 15 metres long (49 ft) that stretches diagonally from floor to ceiling through the installation space. The cables are connected to a real-time sound-synthesis server sending data to the internet. Conceived as a worldwide musical communication piece, it allows participants from different locations to collaborate by plucking or pulling strings. Sound data is then streamed to each site and video projections provide a visual connection among the users.

MUSICIANS ARE THRILL-SEEKERS, LOOKING FOR INTENSITY AND EXCITEMENT IN PERFORMING. WE SEEK TO TRANSMIT THIS FEELING TO THE LISTENER, TO PULL THEM IN AND SURROUND THEM WITH THE SENSATION WE EXPERIENCE MAKING MUSIC. IN THE END, THE VISITORS PLAYING THE INSTALLATION FORGET THE DIGITAL BACKBONE OF THE WORK. INSTEAD, THEY ARE SURROUNDED BY THE ORGANIC FREQUENCIES PULSING THE AIR, AND THIS IS THE SOUND OF THE LARGER-THAN-LIFE ELECTRIC GUITAR STRING THAT THEY GRASP IN THEIR HANDS, AND THAT DEPARTS INTO THE ETHER, INTO THE HANDS OF A REMOTE PARTNER.
ATAU TANAKA AND KASPER TOEPLITZ

PETER TEREZAKIS, *L'AUTRE ('THE OTHER')*,
1996. SOUND INSTALLATION,
2.4 X 5.6 X 0.3 M (8 X 18 X 1 FT)
Viewers create sounds by interacting with this sculpture
within a saturated colour field. The intersections of the
steel grid contain sensors and by moving one's shadow
over them, different sounds are triggered. The work
has also been accompanied by a dance performance.

I THINK OF MYSELF MORE AS AN ANALOGUE THAN A DIGITAL ARTIST. AT THE SAME TIME, I HAVE GREATLY BENEFITED FROM THE FLEXIBILITY AND IMMEDIACY OF DIGITAL MEDIA'S EDITING, STORAGE AND PROCESSING POTENTIAL. MAYBE IT'S BETTER TO SAY I HAVE DONE MY BEST TO KEEP A HEALTHY TENSION BETWEEN ANALOGUE CIRCUITRY AND DIGITAL TOOLS.
STEPHEN VITIELLO

Left
STEPHEN VITIELLO, *WORLD TRADE CENTER RECORDINGS: WINDS AFTER HURRICANE FLOYD*, 1999. MIXED-MEDIA SOUND INSTALLATION
This installation began with two microphones taped to the inside of windows at the World Trade Center in New York. The sounds – which included passing planes and helicopters, traffic, and the noise of the building swaying in the post-hurricane wind – were recorded during Stephen Vitiello's six-month participation in the World Views Artist Residency Program. They were later played back in a darkened gallery.

Opposite
STEPHEN VITIELLO, *FROGS IN FEEDBACK*, 2002. MICROPHONE, GLITTER-BALL MOTOR, SPEAKER, DIGITAL PROCESSOR
Stephen Vitiello takes components that both record and reproduce sounds and uses them as sculptural elements to define the atmosphere of an environment. Here, the slow, mechanical rotation of a microphone over a speaker cone produces feedback of varying pitch and intensity that seems to emanate from the gallery's walls and windows.

DIGITAL ANIMATION AND VIDEO

Artists who use time-based media in the 21st century have technologies at their disposal that could hardly have been dreamed of only a few decades ago. Professional production tools are now available for the desktop computer, and the ease with which artworks can be formatted for DVD or for online presentation means that access to international distribution channels is readily available. In addition, venues for time-based media have expanded to include not only theatres, museums and galleries, but also the internet and a host of new festivals that celebrate independent animation and video.

To realize a film or an animated work in the pre-digital age was difficult. Traditional animation is a very time-consuming process that requires thousands of drawings to produce even a short work. Film runs through a projector at 24 frames per second, or 1,440 images per minute. Apply this rate to a ten-minute piece, and you can begin to understand the daunting challenge involved in creating hand-drawn animation – then add all the sketches, storyboards and other preliminary drawings needed to develop the project. Owing to the amount of work required, there were very few individuals creating animation as a fine art medium compared to today. Léopold Survage, Hans Richter, Oskar Fischinger and Len Lye are a few of the producers of early experimental animation. Similarly, the number of artists who could work in the medium of live-action film was limited by the cost of purchasing raw stock, making projection prints and hiring equipment and crews. In spite of these obstacles, experimental and creative work dating from the early 1900s exists in the archives of the Smithsonian American Art Museum in Washington, DC, as well as the Museum of Modern Art in New York (MoMA), among others.

As with most technology-based art forms, video art is generally agreed to have begun with an invention – in this case the Sony Portapak portable video camera, which was released in 1965. One of the first artists to purchase it was Nam June Paik, who is widely considered the father of video art. Woody and Steina Vasulka founded The Kitchen in New York in 1971, which began as an artists' collective and has since become a major centre for video, music, dance, performance, film and literature, as well as maintaining an extensive archive. Laurie Anderson and Bill Viola are examples of established artists who made the transition into digital media from backgrounds in video, performance and other traditional art practices.

The techniques of digital animation and video art

Digital emulation has allowed most creative processes to be performed on a personal computer rather than in a post-production studio. Computer animators often use a combination of animation software with other digital video programmes to produce their work, a mix that has given rise to a new visual aesthetic. Some artists who create two-dimensional animation incorporate photographic images and video into their work, and even those who employ the traditional hand-drawn approach find that digital technology offers new possibilities. The animator who draws by hand can scan his or her designs into the computer and then use software applications such as Adobe Photoshop or Corel Painter to add colour. The final sequence of images is then imported into a two-dimensional animation programme such as Adobe After Effects, which is used to composite, animate and layer visual effects. These applications can accommodate most types of source material, from stills and text to digitized film footage, and allow the artist to work at any resolution, from film-quality to standard-definition video. The animator is able to play back, adjust and review the animation until he or she is satisfied with it, whereupon the work is output to a digital video file or DVD. Animators who work with three-dimensional software often choose packages such as Alias Maya, Avid Softimage, NewTek LightWave or Autodesk 3ds Max – applications that offer a huge range of capabilities (as anyone who has seen a recent three-dimensional animated feature film or video game can confirm). Video artists working with live action first digitize the footage into a computer and then edit it using non-linear editing software such as Apple Final Cut Pro or Adobe Premiere Pro. Whichever creative and production processes are used, digital animation and video artists can now – through the evolution of technology – achieve professional, high-quality results on desktop computers.

The practitioners

Two innovators of computer animation are Larry Cuba and Karl Sims. Beginning in 1974, Cuba employed computer programming to create abstract animations, and his work could also be considered a type of 'visual music' given the intimate relationship he creates between sound and image. Sims is known for his work in the development of particle systems – dynamic computer graphics that simulate natural phenomena such as water flows, fire, smoke and rain through computer algorithms. 'To animate' means 'to give life to', and Sims's *Panspermia* (pp. 160–61), produced in 1990, was instrumental in establishing computer programming as a new and valid method of animation – moving it from a traditional, hand-animated, team-designed narrative medium to an art form produced by an individual. Yoichiro Kawaguchi also incorporates elements of artificial life in his work (pp. 152–53). Dennis H. Miller uses programming, but in an intimate relationship with music to create his animation (pp. 154–55); Wayne Lytle takes this concept even further with his MIDI-driven musical instruments, which are the central characters in his work (pp. 156–57). A very different approach is taken by Clara Chan in *Autumn Bamboo* (opposite), in which she has chosen to retain the traditional aesthetic of Chinese painting while adding the modern dimension of animation. Toni Dove explores the concepts of alternative cinema, not only through her approach to plot and narrative, but also through the incorporation of her work into interactive environments (pp. 150–51); and Jim Campbell's methods include image-processing techniques, installation, surveillance and even the incorporation of the gallery visitor into the video artwork (pp. 16, 146).

Works that incorporate video and animation into net art, software and other digital art forms can be found in other chapters. In addition, a multitude of annual festivals held around the world offer the opportunity to view independent digital animation and video, and there are several specialized venues. Of particular note are the annual ACM SIGGRAPH conference in the United States; the Ars Electronica Centre in Linz, Austria; Zentrum für Kunst und Medientechnologie Karlsruhe (ZKM), Germany; Inter-Society for the Electronic Arts (ISEA); the New York Digital Salon; and the RESFEST travelling digital film festival.

The works that follow reflect the diversity of time-based media and have been chosen for their historical significance, the artist's unique approach, or because they constitute a landmark within the landscape of digital animation and video art.

**CLARA CHAN, *AUTUMN BAMBOO*, 2000.
COMPUTER ANIMATION**
Chinese brush painting has existed for thousands of
years and is defined by strict stylistic standards. In this
brief but beautifully contemplative work, Clara Chan
has brought the art form to life, so that the viewer
seems to move between the bamboo stems. At the last
moment, the scene is revealed as a painting on a fan,
which snaps shut. The final look was achieved through
creating procedural shaders using the Renderman
programming language and Maya software.

Left
JIM CAMPBELL, *CHURCH ON FIFTH AVENUE*, 2001. CUSTOM ELECTRONICS, 768 LEDS, TREATED PLEXIGLAS MATERIAL, 55.9 X 73.7 X 16.5 CM (22 X 29 X 6½ IN)
This piece consists of a 32 x 24 matrix of computer-controlled red LEDs, which show images of pedestrians and traffic in Manhattan derived from video footage. In front of the grid stands an angled piece of Plexiglas, which, depending on its distance from the LEDs, seems to convert the pixellated, digital image into a smooth-edged, analogue one.

Below left
JIM CAMPBELL, *MOTION AND REST #5 (WHITE)*, 2002. CUSTOM ELECTRONICS, 768 LEDS, 55.9 X 73.7 X 16.5 CM (22 X 29 X 6½ IN)
Jim Campbell used Eadweard Muybridge's 19th-century photographs as one of the inspirations for the series of works entitled *Motion and Rest*. His purpose is to focus on the walking movement of a disabled person, using very low resolution to remove all other personal traits.

MY WORK INCORPORATES ELECTRONIC MEMORY, PRERECORDED IMAGES AND LIVE IMAGES. USING TECHNOLOGICAL TOOLS AND SCIENTIFIC MODELS AS METAPHORS FOR MEMORY AND ILLUSION, MY WORK SEEKS TO INTERPRET, REPRESENT AND MIRROR PSYCHOLOGICAL STATES AND PROCESSES AND THEIR BREAKDOWN. TIME AND MEMORY, INDIVIDUAL AND COLLECTIVE, ELECTRONIC AND REAL, ARE THE ELEMENTS OF MY WORK.
JIM CAMPBELL

CORY ARCANGEL, *URBANDALE*, 2001. DIGITAL MOVIE
This film by Cory Arcangel – perhaps best known for his work with out-of-date computer hardware – was shot at a shopping mall in the suburbs of Buffalo, New York, and provides a stark picture of relentless urban sprawl. The footage was converted into various bitmapped formats and placed on the internet, a process that lends the video an abstract, animated appearance. It features a musical score by Arcangel played on multiple electric guitars.

BY WRITING MY OWN SOFTWARE, I CAN BE IN CONTROL OF EVERY AESTHETIC DECISION OF MY WORK, AND BY WRITING FOR COMPUTERS SOMETIMES FIFTEEN TO TWENTY YEARS OLD, I CAN BE ASSURED THAT THE SIMPLIFIED ARCHITECTURE OF THESE MACHINES WILL PROVIDE ME WITH FREEDOM FOR ARTISTIC EXPRESSION.
CORY ARCANGEL

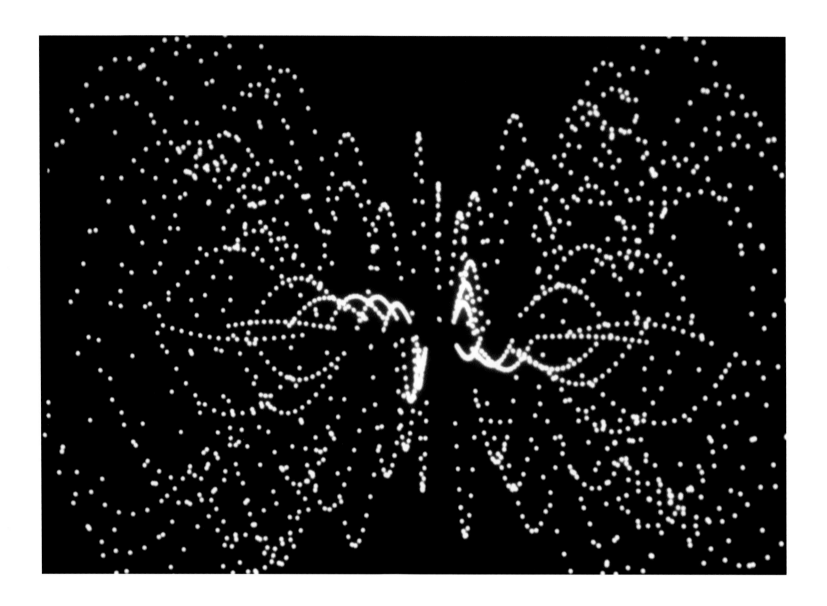

WRITING COMPUTER CODE IS CREATING A PATTERN THAT CREATES PATTERN. AN UNPREDICTABLE VISUAL COMPOSITION EMERGES FROM A MATHEMATICAL STRUCTURE. I COLLABORATE WITH AN ANIMATION-PRODUCING ROBOT WHOSE BEHAVIOUR I DESIGN. OVER TIME THE ALGORITHMS, IMAGERY AND ARTIST COEVOLVE.
LARRY CUBA

Above
DENNIS H. MILLER, *FAKTURA 2*, 2003. COMPUTER ANIMATION
Dennis H. Miller came to visual art and animation from a background
as a composer and brings elements of a musical aesthetic to his work in
the form of repetitive, rhythmic patterns of movement. The visual material
of *Faktura 2* was created with the POV-Ray (persistance of vision ray
tracer) scene description language. Its techniques include the morphing of
iso-surfaces and the application of control parameters extracted from pre-
existing sequences of bitmap files to control the motion of new, synthetic
images.

Opposite
DENNIS H. MILLER, *VIS A VIS*, 2002. COMPUTER ANIMATION
Vis a Vis combines music and imagery that share a number of governing
principles, both technical and formal. A grid-like image might be
superimposed over a swirling, amorphous background, while the
accompanying music makes use of a similar 'contrapuntal' configuration.
Continuity is achieved through a series of variations on the visual and
musical motifs that opened the piece.

UNLIKE SOME MIXED-MEDIA WORKS, WHERE THE PARAMETERS OF THE MUSIC
DIRECTLY CONTROL ASPECTS OF THE PICTURE (OR VICE VERSA), I VIEW MUSIC
AND ANIMATION AS TWO SEPARATE BUT EQUAL STREAMS THAT HAPPEN TO
COEXIST IN THE SAME TIME FRAME. MY GOAL IS TO APPLY THE SAME PRINCIPLES
OF CONTINUITY AND DEVELOPMENT TO THE VISUAL AND MUSICAL ELEMENTS;
IN OTHER WORDS, TO UNIFY THE WORKS BY MAKING THEMATIC CONNECTIONS
THAT ARE MORE OR LESS TRANSPARENT TO THE VIEWER.
DENNIS H. MILLER

WAYNE LYTLE, *PIPE DREAM* **FROM** *ANIMUSIC***, 2001.**
DVD ANIMATION
Created by animator and musician Wayne Lytle, *Animusic* is a series of
3D works in which highly imaginative, self-performing instruments play
a MIDI soundtrack. In *Pipe Dream* an organ-like mechanism is activated
by bouncing balls; *Harmonic Voltage* includes a collection of elaborate
percussive instruments and pulsing lights; and *Acoustic Curves* features
an instrument that reminds one of a hammered dulcimer, along with
mechanical drums and virtual tubular bells. The perfect synchronization
between animation and music is accomplished through MIDIMotion,
a motion-generation software that uses data provided by the MIDI music
files to activate the instruments.

Above
WAYNE LYTLE, *HARMONIC VOLTAGE* **FROM** *ANIMUSIC***, 2001.**
DVD ANIMATION

Opposite
WAYNE LYTLE, *ACOUSTIC CURVES* **FROM** *ANIMUSIC***, 2001.**
DVD ANIMATION

**WE ARE VIRTUAL MUSICAL INSTRUMENT BUILDERS. WE CHOSE TO WORK IN THE
DIGITAL REALM SINCE IT IS IMPOSSIBLE TO BUILD REAL WORKING VERSIONS OF
THESE INSTRUMENTS. THEY CAN ONLY EXIST IN THE COMPUTER. WE ARE ABLE TO
MAKE CHANGES TO ANY ASPECT, EVEN FUNDAMENTAL CHANGES IN THE DESIGN
OR BEHAVIOUR, RIGHT UP TO THE POINT OF PRESSING THE 'RENDER BUTTON'.**
WAYNE LYTLE

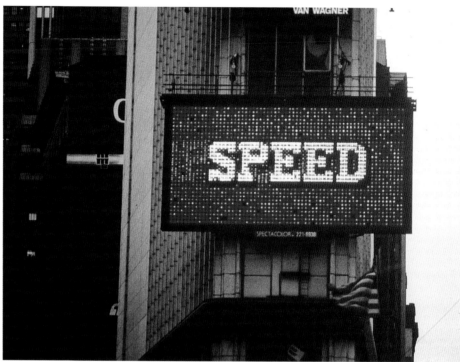

MUNTADAS, *THIS IS NOT AN ADVERTISEMENT*, 1985. SPECTACOLOR ELECTRONIC BILLBOARD, TIMES SQUARE, NEW YORK

These works were part of a series called *Messages to the Public*, for which numerous artists (including Jenny Holzer, Keith Haring and David Hammonds) were commissioned by New York's Public Art Fund to create works for the Spectacolor electronic billboard. *THIS IS NOT AN ADVERTISEMENT* was an animated sequence of words that included: 'THIS IS NOT AN ADVERTISEMENT', 'THIS IS AN ADVERTISEMENT', 'SUBLIMINAL', 'FRAGMENTATION' and 'SPEED'. Muntadas is known for creating artworks that address the relationship between public and private spaces, and the issues of censorship and access to information (p. 198).

THE STARTING POINT FOR MY WORK IS WHAT I CALL 'RELATION DICHOTOMIES', SUCH AS OBJECTIVE/SUBJECTIVE, PUBLIC/PRIVATE, INTERIOR/EXTERIOR. THESE EXTREMES FURNISH ME WITH THE CREATION OF A STRUCTURE. THEY ARE LIKE SETS OF STEREOTYPES, BUT WHAT INTERESTS ME IS THE BETWEEN, WHAT'S BEHIND, WHAT LIES HIDDEN.
MUNTADAS

**KARL SIMS, *PARTICLE DREAMS*, 1988.
COMPUTER ANIMATION**

Particle Dreams is a collection of 'dream sequences'
developed using 3D particle-system software, and
includes an animated human head and environments
such as a waterfall and a snowstorm. A recipient of
a MacArthur Fellowship Award in 1998, Karl Sims
was a pioneer in the development of artificial life and
evolutionary software systems.

I ATTEMPTED TO UNITE SEVERAL CONCEPTS: CHAOS, COMPLEXITY, EVOLUTION, SELF-PROPAGATING ENTITIES AND THE NATURE OF LIFE ITSELF. THIS BOTANICAL FORM OF LIFE, REPRODUCING ITSELF FROM PLANET TO PLANET THROUGH SPACE, IS IN MANY WAYS ANALOGOUS TO OTHER SELF-REPLICATING SYSTEMS, INCLUDING ORGANISMS, ENTIRE SPECIES OR EVEN IDEAS. A WINDOW INTO THIS SYSTEM, REPLICATING ON A GRANDER SCALE, IS MEANT TO INCREASE AWARENESS OF SELF-PROPAGATING SYSTEMS IN GENERAL, AS WELL AS INSPIRE THOUGHTS ABOUT OUR ENTIRE PLANET.
KARL SIMS

KARL SIMS, *PANSPERMIA*, 1990. COMPUTER ANIMATION
Panspermia portrays the life cycle of an imaginary intergalactic life form.
From the opening sequence, which shows the arrival of a seed pod on
a planet's surface, we see the plants begin to grow and take adult form,
develop into a forest and finally launch more spores into space,
beginning the process anew. Karl Sims used original software to create
and animate the 3D plant structures.

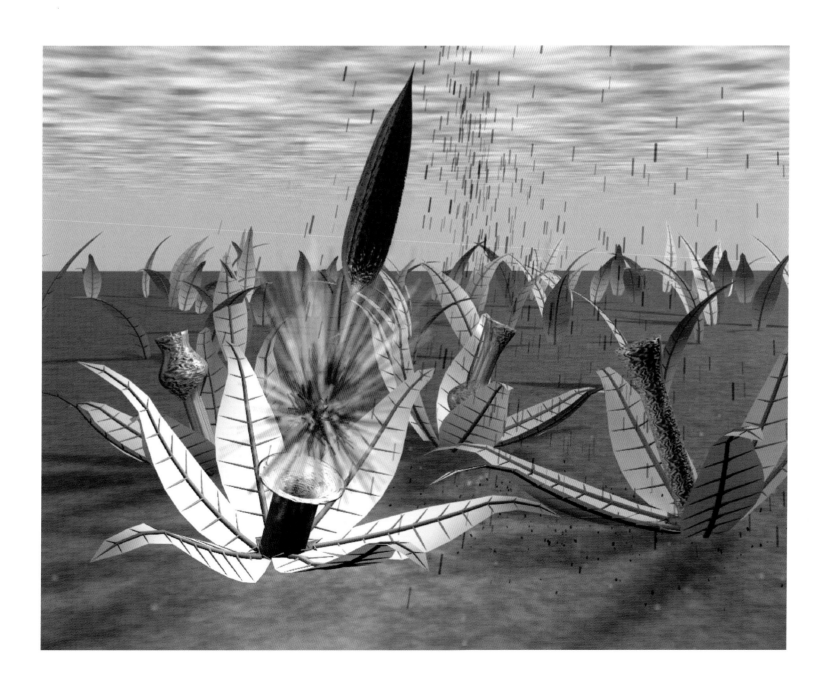

IT IS FROM NATURE THAT I DRAW MY INSPIRATION, AND NATURE IS THE VERY ELEMENT THAT DOMINATES MY WORK. I ENJOY AND SPEND TIME WATCHING THE CLOUDS OR THE GLOWING REFLECTIONS ON PLANTS; AND WHEN I WORK I LET ALL THE IMAGES I HAVE ABSORBED EMERGE THROUGH MY MEMORY.
OPY ZOUNI

Opposite
OPY ZOUNI, *ART AND INDUSTRIAL PRODUCT*, 2004. DIGITAL VIDEO

Left
OPY ZOUNI, *LIGHT/SHADOW/ COINCIDENCES*, 1999. DIGITAL VIDEO

Below left
OPY ZOUNI, *ART AND CAR*, 2003. DIGITAL VIDEO
In her video pieces, Opy Zouni uses optical phenomena, symmetry and geometry, often observed from nature, to create a very minimal aesthetic. She cites the Bauhaus art movement as a significant influence on her work.

SOFTWARE, DATABASE AND GAME ART

While art forms such as prints, sculpture and even installation evolved from traditional media and techniques, software, database and game art came into existence only when artists started experimenting with computers. There is a fine line between where art that has a primary component of software ends and other categories begin. For example, an artist can write a software programme and then output the artwork as a print or sculpture, or include it in an interactive installation. Every type of digital art makes use of software in some form. For the purposes of this exploration, software art is defined as creative work that finds its origins in programmes written by the artist; database art relies on pre-existing, created or real-time collections of information; and game art uses commercial gaming software or incorporates elements of play and role-playing. Networked games are a hybrid between game art and net art.

Software art finds its primary expression in computer code. Artist and programmer John F. Simon, Jr., likes to refer to programming as a form of creative writing, in which the artist's 'words' exist as lines of code; others have called it the 'paint and canvas' of the digital artist. With *Every Icon* (p. 171), Simon produced an almost endless series of visual images on a 32 x 32 grid, all powered by the algorithms of computer code. While Simon's work is self-generating, Golan Levin's approach to software art in his Audiovisual Environment Suite (pp. 172–73) gives creative control to the user through a minimal interface that produces abstract visual images, animations and sound in real time. Levin describes his work as an 'attempt to reclaim computation as a personal medium of expression'.

A third type of software art has been employed by Alexander R. Galloway (pp. 168, 202) and the Radical Software Group. Carnivore was originally designed as a multi-purpose surveillance tool for data networks, inspired by software the FBI used under the nickname 'Carnivore' to perform electronic wiretaps. *CarnivorePE* (p. 168) is the resultant software application that monitors all internet traffic (email, web surfing) from a specific local network and then puts this data in a form that can be creatively interpreted in any number of ways by other artists. These interpretations, called 'clients', take the form of image and sound generators, or works that utilize breath interfaces; one work by Golan Levin, *JJ*, translates the emotional meaning of words that travel over a network into facial expressions.

While software art embodies the concept of authorship of the software code, database artists take a more interpretative approach through collections of data that exist on disk, the internet, derive from other sources, or are created by the participants and viewers of the artwork itself. A major concern for artists creating database art is to filter, chart or 'map' the information, to visualize it and make it meaningful for an audience. In *Pockets Full of Memories* (pp. 175–77), George Legrady involves the audience in the creation of the database, inviting them to scan their personal possessions and then to ponder the concept of a communal archive and the way in which collective memory functions. Marek Walczak and Martin Wattenberg's *Apartment* (pp. 178–79) encourages participants to create their own database of words, which the software visualizes with an architectural blueprint.

An example of a database artwork that uses real-time stock market data from the internet is Lynn Hershman Leeson's *Synthia* (p. 167). Josh On is similarly concerned with market forces, but in a more people-oriented way: *They Rule* (p. 169) is piece of net art that allows users to trace graphically the relationships between board members of various American corporations. W. Bradford Paley (pp. 182–83) writes software that analyses works of literature and other texts and creates a visual interpretation of patterns hidden within the data. In her works *American Views: Stories of the Landscape* (p. 169) and *NYC Thought Pictures: Memories of Place*, Russet Lederman presents a non-linear collage of the American landscape as seen through the experiences and memories of diverse individuals. These works are accomplished through the development of databases that contain images, sound and text.

The creative interplay between artists and games came to public prominence in 2001 with 'Game Show', exhibited at the Massachusetts Museum of Contemporary Art. Positioned as the first major exhibition to explore how artists have incorporated game structures and themes in their work, the show was composed of four sections: Games Visitors Play, Games Artists Play, Games Artists Orchestrate and Net Games Now, which was curated by Mark Tribe and Alexander R. Galloway of Rhizome.org. This section included *SOD* by Jodi, and *Jackpot* by Maciej Wisniewski. Jodi (pp. 188–89) and Wisnieski (pp. 200–01) are artists who straddle the borders between game art, net art and installation. In their first American exhibition, 'INSTALL.EXE' at Eyebeam in New York, Jodi included several games, such as UNTITLED GAME and CTRL-SPACE, both 'game mods' (game modifications) of Quake 1 (p. 188). Kathleen Ruiz also brings games into a gallery environment with *Bang, Bang (you're not dead?)*, an interactive multi-media game installation (p. 180). Game interactivity relies on player involvement and encourages group cooperation and problem solving. Just as video games span a wide variety of genres – from violent 'shooters' and action games to simulators and 'God games' – so, too, have digital artists chosen different aspects of the gaming world to explore their own themes and concerns. Cory Arcangel hacked into Nintendo cartridges to create *I Shot Andy Warhol* (p. 180), while other works are more abstract and contemplative. The popularity of games has led software companies to invest heavily in their development, and games routinely display innovative design, architectural spaces, virtual environments and myriad narrative constructs, all of which are of interest to game artists.

The working environment of software, database and game artists
Artists who create this type of art find themselves in a very different situation from artists such as digital sculptors or print artists, who exclusively use off-the-shelf software packages. One factor these artists have to consider when creating their work is the final form of expression. For example, work that uses the internet for exhibition, accessing or collecting data requires the use of the appropriate software environment. Likewise, game artists develop their work from pre-existing game engines, such as UNREAL, or by modifying commercially released products. Database artists use software that can archive and access databases, such as MySQL and Macromedia Director. Software artists also use a wide variety of programming languages such as C, C++, Java and Visual Basic. Others take off-the-shelf software further by using the programming and scripting languages embedded in the software application. For example, Macromedia Director includes the programming language Lingo, and Flash has Flash ActionScript. The following works represent new territories of creativity for artists who are working with new modes of expression.

LYNN HERSHMAN LEESON, *SYNTHIA*, 2000–02. NETWORK INSTALLATION, 167.6 X 88.9 CM (66 X 35 IN)

Synthia combines real-time streaming data from the stock market and 3D animation and video modules within a sculptural work that resembles an old Edison stock ticker. The piece is named after its animated character who exhibits different behaviours depending on stock market activity. For example, if the market is up, Synthia dances; if the market is flat, she goes to bed; and if the market goes down, she chain smokes and becomes depressed.

THE BIGGEST CULTURAL RAMIFICATION I SEE IS THAT SOFTWARE IS AN ACTION MEDIUM. SOFTWARE DOES STUFF. THIS IS ENTIRELY DIFFERENT FROM LITERATURE, FILM, OR OTHER PREVIOUS MEDIA. FRIEDRICH A. KITTLER HAS SUMMARIZED THIS POINT BY WRITING THAT CODE IS THE FIRST TYPE OF LANGUAGE THAT DOES WHAT IT SAYS. I AGREE WITH HIM. SOFTWARE IS A TYPE OF MACHINE FOR CONVERTING MEANING INTO ACTION.
ALEXANDER R. GALLOWAY

ALEXANDER R. GALLOWAY AND RSG, *CARNIVORE PE*, 2001. SOFTWARE
This is the Macintosh version of the *CarnivorePE* (Personal Edition) interface, which monitors the flow of data over a specific network. The number of packets of data that are output per second can be counted and can vary. The data format can also be defined. It has a security option to allow clients from other computers to connect or prevent them from doing so. The Radical Software Group (RSG) is an international collective of various programmers and artists who write and work with experimental software. Artists who have incorporated RSG's software in their artworks include Jonah Brucker-Cohen, Vuk Cosic, Joshua Davis, Entropy8Zuper!, Golan Levin and Mark Napier.

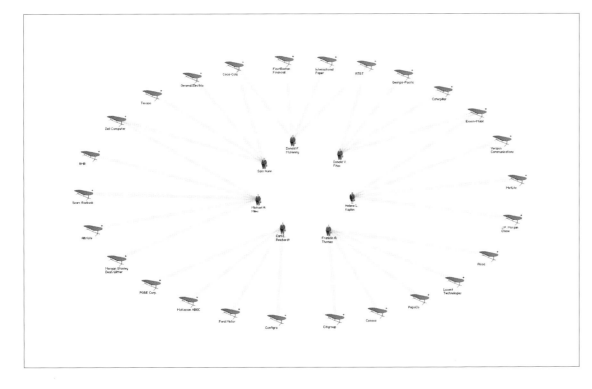

RUSSET LEDERMAN, *AMERICAN VIEWS: STORIES OF THE LANDSCAPE*, 2001. ONLINE ARTWORK

American Views is a series of interactive stories that was commissioned by the Smithsonian American Art Museum. The three main characters are Cindi Cusick, a digital designer from Kentucky; Adam Klein, an environmental engineer from California; and Neil Duskis, a Long Island suburbanite. Through text, audio and graphics, random portions of each character's story are presented in relation to the work's four main themes: seen[scene], permanence [im]permanence, earth[un]earth and use[re]use. A larger perspective of the American cultural landscape is gained through experiencing the stories of these characters.

JOSH ON, *THEY RULE*, 2001. ONLINE ARTWORK. MAP CREATED BY CHRIS MACGREGOR

Political activism has often played a very visible part in contemporary art. In *They Rule*, Josh On states his case with subtle eloquence. This online artwork lets users create graphic maps showing the links between individuals who sit on the board of directors of various prominent corporations. The resulting patterns expose some not-so-obvious connections, revealing the inner structure of corporate governance and providing a unique glimpse of what the artist refers to as the 'U.S. ruling class'. A large collection of these maps are available at www.theyrule.net.

Above
JOHN F. SIMON, JR., *COLOR PANEL v1.0* (INSTALLATION VIEW), 1999. SOFTWARE, MACINTOSH 280C COMPUTERS, ACRYLIC PLASTIC, 36.8 X 26.7 X 8.9 CM (14½ X 10½ X 3½ IN)

Left
JOHN F. SIMON, JR., *COMPLEXCITY*, 2000. SOFTWARE, MACINTOSH POWERBOOK G3, ACRYLIC PLASTIC, 48.3 X 40.6 X 7.6 CM (19 X 16 X 3 IN)

Opposite
JOHN F. SIMON, JR., *EVERY ICON*, 1996. SOFTWARE. ALSO EXHIBITED AS A PROJECTION, APPLET, PALM PILOT APPLICATION AND WALL HANGING LCD PANEL USING APPLE POWERBOOK G3

John F. Simon uses programming as an activated extension of language and considers the patterns and movement that emerge from his original software compositions to be analogous to creative writing. Influenced by Bauhaus artists Kandinsky and Klee, *Color Panel v1.0* is a time-based study that interprets colour conventions into software, resulting in a dynamic composition of changing palettes. This installation of *Color Panel* shows twelve laptops that have been modified into 'art appliances' (a term coined by Simon), transforming the LCD screen and internal components into a virtual canvas *and* an art object. *ComplexCity* is an animated modern-day cityscape that documents the artist's relationship with New York, and is reminiscent of Mondrian's *Broadway Boogie Woogie*. While these works are based on objects shown in a gallery, *Every Icon* began as an internet artwork and was influential in defining the nature of software art, gaining critical acclaim from the *New York Times* for its conceptual approach.

EVERY ICON IS A PIECE OF CONCEPTUAL ART REALIZED IN SOFTWARE THAT HAS BEEN PRESENTED AS AN ONLINE INSTALLATION, A PALM PILOT APPLICATION AND A SELF-CONTAINED WALL HANGING OBJECT. THE PIECE CONSISTS OF A 32 X 32 SQUARE GRID WHERE EVERY SQUARE CAN BE COLOURED BLACK OR WHITE. *EVERY ICON* STARTS WITH AN IMAGE WHERE EVERY SQUARE IS WHITE AND PROGRESSES THROUGH COMBINATIONS OF BLACK AND WHITE SQUARES UNTIL EVERY SQUARE IS BLACK. THE PIECE WILL SHOW EVERY POSSIBLE IMAGE. ALTHOUGH IT TAKES ONLY 1.36 YEARS TO DISPLAY ALL OF THE VARIATIONS ALONG THE FIRST LINE BY SHOWING ONE HUNDRED ICONS PER SECOND, IT TAKES AN EXPONENTIALLY LONGER 5.85 BILLION YEARS TO COMPLETE THE SECOND LINE. EVEN IN THIS LIMITED VISUAL SPACE, THERE ARE MORE IMAGES THAN THE HUMAN MIND CAN EXPERIENCE IN MANY LIFETIMES. IN THIS WAY THE PIECE COMMENTS ON THE PROMISE OF TECHNOLOGY.

JOHN F. SIMON, JR.

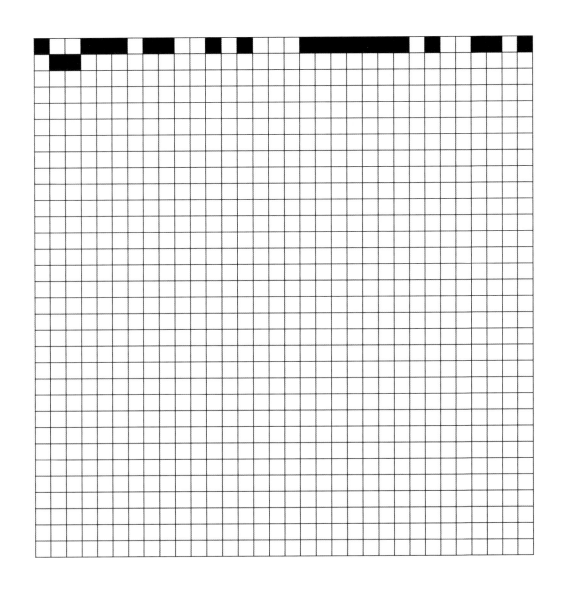

Given:
An Icon described by a 32 X 32 Grid

Allowed:
Any element of the grid to be colored black or white.

Shown:
Every Icon

Owner:
John F. Simon, Jr.

Edition Number:
Artist's Proof

Starting Time:
January 14, 1997, 9:00:00 pm

Opposite above and below
GOLAN LEVIN, *FLOCCUS* AND *YELLOWTAIL,* 1999.
INTERACTIVE SOFTWARE
Floccus and *Yellowtail* are components of the Audiovisual Environment
Suite, a set of interactive software systems designed so that people can
create abstract animations and synthetic sounds in real-time. In a typical
installation of these works, a pedestal with a computer mouse on top is
positioned in the centre of a darkened room, and a video projector
displays a large image on one of the walls. The software interface is
simple and intuitive, and within a short period of time users are creating
a wide variety of abstract visuals and sounds. An interesting aspect of
Golan Levin's work is that each person who uses the software ends up
with his or her own unique visuals.

Below
GOLAN LEVIN, SCOTT GIBBONS AND GREGORY SHAKAR,
***SCRIBBLE,* 2000. NEW MEDIA PERFORMANCE AT ARS**
ELECTRONICA, LINZ, AUSTRIA
This image shows a concert performance of *Scribble*, also produced
through the Audiovisual Environment Suite. The work revives and updates
a decades-old tradition of kinetic light performance, featuring tightly
coupled sounds and dynamic visuals that are at times carefully scored,
and at other times loosely improvized.

**IN *FLOCCUS*, DUCTILE FILAMENTS
DRAWN BY THE USER SWIRL AROUND
A SHIFTING, IMAGINARY DRAIN
CENTRED AT THE USER'S CURSOR.
THESE FILAMENTS ARE TORN BY
CONFLICTING IMPULSES TO
SIMULTANEOUSLY PRESERVE THEIR
LENGTH, YET ALSO MOVE TOWARDS
OR AWAY FROM THE CURSOR. THEY
FIND AN EQUILIBRIUM BY FORMING
GNARLY, TANGLED MASSES.**
GOLAN LEVIN

MICHAEL FIELD, *ARMIES OF THE NIGHT*, 2000.
DURST LAMBDA PRINT, 86.3 X 86.3 CM (34 X 34 IN)
Michael Field relies on the interplay between symmetrical
and chaotic systems in his mathematically generated images,
focusing on the underlying structure that can sometimes be
concealed by chaos. Colour, movement and illusion are
important elements of his work.

LIFE ITSELF – DEPENDING AS IT DOES ON THE STATISTICAL LAWS OF GENETICS AND INHERITANCE – IS MAYBE THE BEST AND MOST FAMILIAR EXPRESSION OF THE ROLE THAT RANDOMNESS PLAYS IN OUR EXISTENCE. VIEWED IN THIS LIGHT, RANDOMNESS COEXISTS WITH AND ILLUMINATES FORM AND STRUCTURE – THE OPPOSITE OF THE CONVENTIONAL VIEW THAT CHAOS IS THE ANTITHESIS OF STRUCTURE.
MICHAEL FIELD

Right and overleaf
GEORGE LEGRADY, *POCKETS FULL OF MEMORIES*, 2001. INTERACTIVE INSTALLATION
Visitors to this installation scan their personal possessions at a kiosk and the objects are then categorized according to a software algorithm written by Timo Honkela and Timo Koskenniemi. At the start of the exhibition the database is empty but grows through the public's contributions. The algorithm organizes the data throughout, to arrive at a final ordered state at the end of the exhibition. The phenomenon of proceeding from small local actions (each contribution) to a final ordered state is called 'emergence', since the order emerges over time through the local interactions generated by the algorithm each time a new object enters the database. In this sense, the system has been defined as 'self-organizing'.

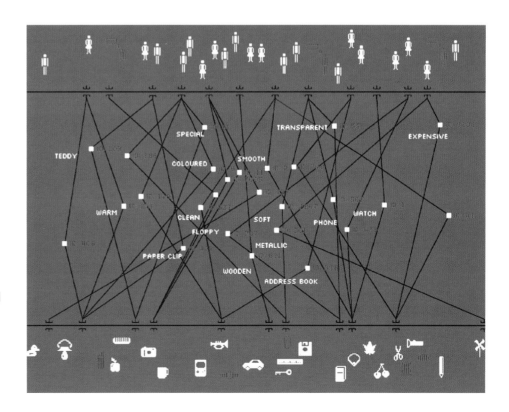

POCKETS FULL OF MEMORIES **IS AN INTERACTIVE INSTALLATION IN WHICH THE PUBLIC CONTRIBUTE AN IMAGE OF AN OBJECT IN THEIR POSSESSION TO AN ARCHIVE THAT GROWS THROUGHOUT THE EXHIBITION. THE DATA IS STORED IN A DATABASE THAT IS PROJECTED LARGE-SCALE IN THE GALLERY AND IS ACCESSIBLE ON THE INTERNET. THE KOHONEN SELF-ORGANIZING MAP ALGORITHM DETERMINES THE LOCATION OF THE OBJECTS BY POSITIONING THEM IN A TWO-DIMENSIONAL MATRIX ACCORDING TO SIMILARITIES DEFINED BY THE CONTRIBUTORS. THE AUDIENCE CAN ALSO INTERACT WITH THE DATA ONLINE TO ACCESS DESCRIPTIONS AND TO CONTRIBUTE COMMENTS.**
GEORGE LEGRADY

177

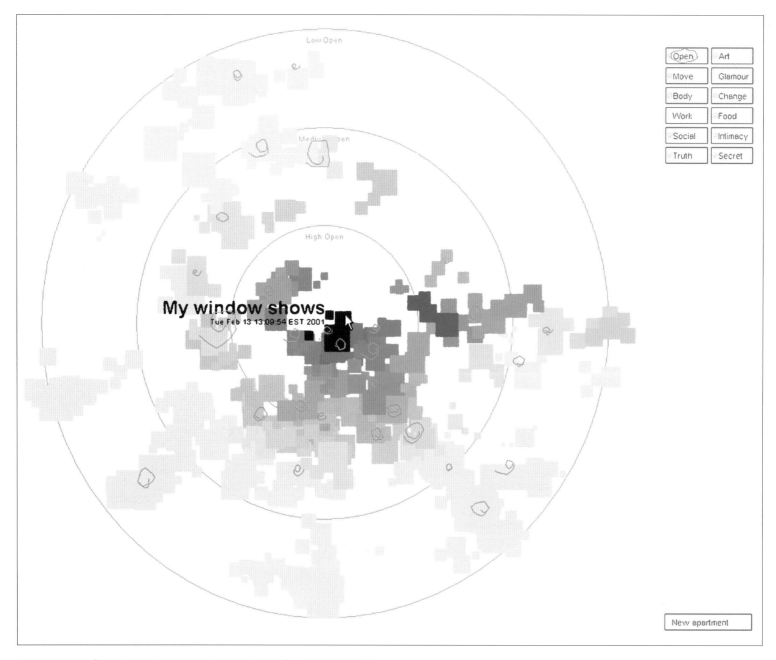

MAREK WALCZAK AND MARTIN WATTENBERG, *APARTMENT*, 2001. WEB- AND INSTALLATION-BASED SOFTWARE, VARIABLE DIMENSIONS

Apartment is an example of database art that requires visitors to the gallery or to the website to create and define the contents of the database. Conceptually, the work is similar in approach to George Legrady's *Pockets Full of Memories* (pp. 176–77); however, in this instance words replace personal items as the fundamental data. Words typed into the computer prompt the appearance of rooms or 'apartments', the architecture of which is determined by the computer's analysis. The apartments are then converted into navigable 3D environments composed of various images.

VIEWERS ARE CONFRONTED WITH A BLINKING CURSOR. AS THEY TYPE, ROOMS
BEGIN TO TAKE SHAPE IN THE FORM OF A TWO-DIMENSIONAL PLAN, SIMILAR
TO A BLUEPRINT. THE ARCHITECTURE IS BASED ON A SEMANTIC ANALYSIS OF THE
VIEWER'S WORDS, REORGANIZED TO REFLECT THE UNDERLYING THEMES THEY
EXPRESS. THE APARTMENTS ARE THEN CLUSTERED INTO BUILDINGS AND CITIES
ACCORDING TO THEIR LINGUISTIC RELATIONSHIPS. IN A MNEMONIC TECHNIQUE,
LONG BEFORE THE 'POST-IT' ERA, CICERO IMAGINED INSCRIBING THE THEMES OF
A SPEECH ON A SUITE OF ROOMS IN A VILLA, AND THEN RECITING THAT SPEECH
BY MENTALLY WALKING FROM SPACE TO SPACE. ESTABLISHING AN EQUIVALENCE
BETWEEN LANGUAGE AND SPACE, *APARTMENT* CONNECTS THE WRITTEN WORD
WITH DIFFERENT FORMS OF SPATIAL CONFIGURATIONS.
MARTIN WALCZAK AND MARTIN WATTENBERG

CORY ARCANGEL, *I SHOT ANDY WARHOL*, 2002. REPROGRAMMED NINTENDO CARTRIDGE

Rather than working within the confines of off-the-shelf software, Cory Arcangel writes his own. For *I Shot Andy Warhol*, the artist took a 1980s video game called Hogan's Alley and replaced the original characters with cultural icons. The object of the game is to shoot Andy Warhol and avoid hitting the other characters, who include Pope John Paul II, Flavor Flav of Public Enemy and Colonel Sanders.

KATHLEEN RUIZ, *BANG, BANG (YOU'RE NOT DEAD?)*, 2000. INTERACTIVE MULTI-MEDIA GAME INSTALLATION, 4.6 X 5.5 X 4.9 M (15 X 18 X 16 FT)

Offering an alterative interactive experience to the 'first-person shooter' video game, the goal of *Bang, Bang (you're not dead?)* is to shoot at people who are already dead and resurrect them. The installation includes large images of teenagers playing these video games and confronting each other with fake guns. The total environment encourages the viewer/participant to reflect upon issues of virtual violence, catharsis and desensitization in simulated space.

Opposite
KATHLEEN RUIZ, *STUNT DUMMIES*, 2003. INTERACTIVE MULTI-MEDIA GAME INSTALLATION, 4.6 X 5.5 X 4.9 M (15 X 18 X 16 FT)

Stunt Dummies questions our relationship with video games and technology, and examines the cultural impact of the digital era on our social interactions, ethics and individual identities. This image shows the menu interface of the work, which allows users to explore seven virtual worlds. Kathleen Ruiz drew her inspiration for the interface from the 15th-century painting *The Seven Deadly Sins and the Four Last Things* by Hieronymus Bosch.

THE COMPUTER IS A WONDERFUL FACILITATOR OF CREATIVE THOUGHT. MORE THAN ANYTHING, DIGITAL MEDIA HELPS ME TO EXPLORE THE CONFLUENCE OF THE IMAGINARY AND THE REAL. I WANT THE OBSERVER TO BECOME A PARTICIPANT IN THESE IDEAS, EXPLORING THE PROMISE OF TECHNOLOGY, AS WELL AS ITS FRIGHTENING, FASCINATING AND HUMOROUS CONTRADICTIONS.
KATHLEEN RUIZ

W. BRADFORD PALEY,
***TEXTARC*, 2002. POSTSCRIPT**
PRINT GENERATED BY
INTERACTIVE TEXT ANALYSIS
TOOL, 86.4 X 53.3 CM
(31 X 21 IN)

W. Bradford Paley describes
this work as a visual index or
concordance of a text. *TextArc*
takes two forms: an online
model (textarc.org) that illustrates
a complete text, for example
a novel, on a single screen; and
the PostScript version, tuned to
the advantages of high-resolution
printing. Words that are used
frequently are larger and brighter,
and the star-like shapes point to
every place a word is used. The
online version also traces the
original word order by means of
a coloured curve. The work allows
one to view a written piece from
a completely new perspective and
is in use at several universities as
a tool for literary research. This
example analyses Lewis Carroll's
Alice in Wonderland.

NET ART

While many digital art forms have their roots in traditional media, net art originates from and exists only in the realm of networked media. Text-based artworks have been created since the early days of the internet; however, it was not until the mid-1990s, when graphical browsers such as Mosaic (1993), Netscape Navigator (1994) and Internet Explorer (1995) became widespread, that net art really took hold as a global art form. The nomenclature surrounding this type of art is still evolving, and net art is also referred to as internet art, networked art and web art. There are many kinds of net art: text-based works; politically motivated net activism; browser art; image sites, which include photographs, drawing and digital images; performance; video and audio works; streaming video works based on surveillance; and, more recently, works created using mobile phones, mobile computing and the Global Positioning System (GPS).

One characteristic of net art is its availability to a global audience. It can reach its viewers through sites that use low bandwidth text and graphics – the most reliable way of obtaining the widest possible access – or through ultra-high bandwidth projects that can be seen and experienced in high-end net art centres. Another advantage of net art is the independence it offers artists, who can exhibit their work outside the conventional venues of museum and gallery. They have tremendous freedom to communicate with their audience directly and to do so in an intimate fashion, since the vast majority of net art is experienced by individuals in their homes. Each viewer's physical involvement through the mouse, keyboard and screen also give the medium interactivity.

The growth of net art has been closely linked to the evolution of the internet and its rapidly evolving technology. The initial ARPANET, a communication network commission by the United States Department of Defense and implemented by four universities, remained largely a research tool until Tim Berners-Lee proposed a global project using hypertext: the World Wide Web. The first website was posted in 1991, and the early web continued to be used by educational and research institutions as a free and largely unregulated means of information-sharing.

Early net art included multi-user domains (MUDs) and multi-user object-oriented experiences (MOOs), which consisted of role-playing games and other text-based interactions. As the internet became capable of disseminating images as well as audio and video streaming, net art experienced a parallel growth. One consequence of this rapid evolution was that a large percentage of early internet art fell victim to browser and software upgrades. The turnaround time for internet software development during the dot.com era of the mid- to late-1990s was as quick as four to six months. Net art projects became obsolete as newer versions of browsers and plug-ins – as well as hardware upgrades – were no longer capable of supporting them. Many museums, non-profit foundations and artists now keep inventories of old computers and discontinued software so that early works can be preserved. New developments in the software emulation of older operating systems and computers can also help to archive these works.

Nettime, founded by Geert Lovink and Pit Schultz in 1995, was established to promote internet culture and criticism, and artists who aided in its formation include Heath Bunting, Vuk Cosic, Jodi, Olia Lialina and Alexei Shulgin. Jodi, the artistic team of Joan Heemskerk and Dirk Paesmans, were well known partially on account of their unique creative work that questioned the fundamental concept of the browser. Around the same time the New York-based Rhizome.org, founded by Mark Tribe, offered an open forum for discussion on net art and also developed an archive. The Walker Art Center Net Art Initiative, founded by Steve Deitz in Minneapolis, was very influential in supporting net art, hosting an important collection and a series of online exhibitions. A number of museum websites, such as the Whitney Museum of American Art Artport, the Solomon R. Guggenheim Museum and the San Francisco Museum of Modern Art, also became net art advocates.

Video-based interaction on the internet began with CUseeMe and MBONE, the video conferencing software that spawned performance-based pieces and other interactive net video works. Since then, video projects – both interactive and linear – have developed rapidly on the web, although they are heavily dependent on ample bandwidth for their success. Currently, organizations such as La Société des Arts Technologiques (SAT) in Montreal and MARCEL, founded by Don Foresta in France, are working with ultra-high bandwidth applications for creative purposes, using networks such as Access Grid (AG), Internet2 and National LambdaRail (NLR).

The advent of wireless technology now allows net artists creative possibilities using mobile handheld devices such as PDAs and mobile phones. Golan Levin's groundbreaking *DIALTONES (A Telesymphony)* at Ars Electronica in 2001 was a concert performed entirely through the ringing of the audience's mobile phones. The Global Positioning System pinpoints the exact position of the viewer through satellite communications. Art projects that use this technology are GPS Drawing, the C5 Landscape Initiative and the Amsterdam RealTime Project. GPS has expanded the definition of net art beyond wired networks, harkening back to the first wireless technology – radio – while looking forward to the wireless environments of the future.

Many museums now have their own net art websites and also commission works for exhibition. The debate as to whether or not net art can be successfully exhibited in museums and galleries is ongoing. Exhibited works that have received wide critical acclaim are Jodi's gallery installations and Wolfgang Staehle's *Empire 24/7*, a time-based work featuring a webcam that documented the 9/11 attacks on New York in 2001. While it is apparent that net art will evolve and grow as an art form, its position in the traditional art establishment will remain in question until it finds a secure place within the broader field of contemporary art.

The net artist's studio

The person who makes net art and the person who views it may use computer technology that is very similar. Since one of the more important aspects of net art is to make it accessible to the largest possible audience, net artists use hardware configurations and software applications that are compatible with their audiences' computers. Ample bandwidth and a high-end computer are the two main requirements of the net artist. High bandwidth greatly increases the possibilities offered by video, audio and interactivity. Access to the highest bandwidth is available in artist-run organizations such as V2 in the Netherlands and ZKM in Germany, as well as through many universities and research facilities. These facilities are limited in number and in availability to the public. Instead, the most widely used high-bandwidth options for net artists and viewers are cable modems and DSL lines. In addition to a high-specification computer, many net artists also employ video and audio devices such as cameras, webcams, MIDI synthesizers, mixing boards and musical instruments. Although off-the-shelf software is sometimes utilized, net artists primarily work with programming languages ranging from basic HTML to the more sophisticated Perl, Java and PHP. While the internet's rate of development has decreased from its frantic pace in the 1990s, its rapid evolution continues to invent unique solutions to the problems of low bandwidth, browser usage, compatibility of programming languages and text differences. Ideally, the net art of the future will be experienced through full-screen video, high-quality multi-channel audio and universal language-translation software. This may seem a long way off, but it is highly likely that these benefits will eventually be enjoyed by the average user and by visitors to museums and galleries.

The practitioners

The freedom net art has afforded its practitioners to reach global audiences has spawned thousands of artists' websites and art projects. The works that follow represent diverse forms of net art and profile such areas as networked video installations, telerobotics, browser art and web art.

Some of the underlying concepts for these artworks were explored as far back as 1977 when Kit Galloway and Sherrie Rabinowitz created *Satellite Arts*, a series of projects that rebelled against the idea of artists simply as end-users of ready-made technologies, and instead viewed them as creative interpreters of emerging technologies. Their best-known work is *Hole-In-Space* (p. 20), described as a 'public communication sculpture' by its creators, which awakened public awareness of telepresence and remote video and audio communication. Later works in the same vein were *Telegarden* (p. 190) by Ken Goldberg – a networked robotic installation that invited participants to plant and water a garden and monitor its growth from remote locations – and *Eliza Redux* (p. 201) by Adrianne Wortzel, which used networked video-streaming technology. Maciej Wisniewski's *netomat*™ (p. 201) expands the browser's interactive capabilities. This type of work, often referred to as 'browser art', is more formal in its aesthetic approach than works that rely on image and text for their content. *StarryNight* (p. 202) by Rhizome.org is both an artistic statement and a unique interface to the Rhizome database. Net activism and the use of net art to foster dialogues on a variety of social issues are represented by Muntadas in *The File Room* (p. 198), which addresses questions of censorship. As one aspect of his artistic practice, Andy Deck encourages web communities to collaborate in the creation of images and drawings (p. 197). Annette Weintraub (p. 203) and Patrick Lichty (p. 199) combine images, video and text in a new form of online narrative. In addition to these projects, other works that employ networked media can be found in the chapters on software, database and game art, and installation and virtual reality. To fully experience net art, readers are encouraged to explore the works themselves on their personal computer using the artists' websites listed at the back of this book.

Above left
JODI, *UNTITLED GAME*, 2000. 13 MODIFICATIONS OF QUAKE 1
Above right
JODI, *CTRL-SPACE*, 1998. MULTI-PLAYER MODIFICATION OF QUAKE 1
Opposite
JODI, *MY%DESKTOP*, 2003. INSTALLATION WITH 4 PROJECTIONS

Joan Heemskerk and Dirk Paesmans, the creative team of Jodi, are perhaps the best known pioneers of net art. From an artistic background that includes photography, video and performance, Jodi produce net art that emulates and comments on technological malfunction: viruses, error messages and computer crashes that turn computer screens into an array of abstract animation and imagery. Their work, often described as technological abstraction, subverts the normal process of navigation with a mouse and keyboard and the traditional interface between human and computer. Their digital artworks have also been presented as CD-ROMs, games and gallery installations.

IT IS OBVIOUS THAT OUR WORK FIGHTS AGAINST HIGH TECH. WE ALSO BATTLE WITH THE COMPUTER ON A GRAPHIC LEVEL. WHEN A VIEWER LOOKS AT OUR WORK, WE ARE INSIDE HIS COMPUTER. YOU ARE VERY CLOSE TO A PERSON WHEN YOU ARE ON HIS OR HER DESKTOP. I THINK THE COMPUTER IS A DEVICE TO GET INTO SOMEONE'S MIND. WE REPLACE THIS MYTHOLOGICAL NOTION OF A VIRTUAL SOCIETY ON THE NET OR WHATEVER WITH OUR OWN WORK. WE PUT OUR OWN PERSONALITY THERE.

JODI

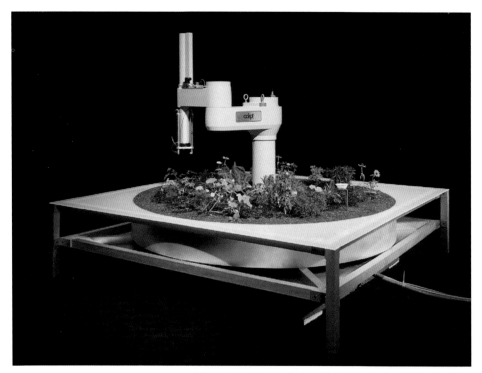

**KEN GOLDBERG, *TELEGARDEN*, 1995–2004 .
NETWORKED ROBOTIC INSTALLATION,
3.7 X 3.7 X 2.4 M (12 X 12 X 8 FT)**

Telegarden was an art installation that allowed web users to view and interact with a remote garden filled with living plants. Visitors could plant, water and monitor the progress of seedlings via the tender administrations of a robotic arm. The common goal of caring for the garden created a sense of community among a widespread network of people. It was one of the earliest examples of telerobotics and boasted more than nine thousand participants during its first year. The installation was moved to the Ars Electronica Center in Linz, Austria, in 1996 and remained operational until 2004.

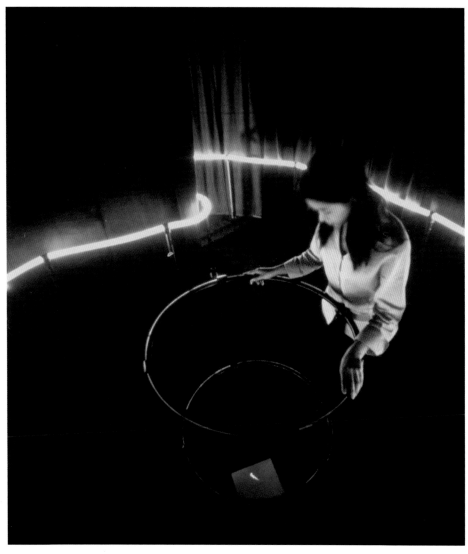

**KEN GOLDBERG, RANDALL PACKER,
GREGORY KUHN AND WOJCIECH MATUSIK,
MORI, 1999. INTERNET-BASED INSTALLATION,
6 X 6 X 30 M (20 X 20 X 10 FT)**

Mori is an immersive installation that connects participants to the vibration of the Earth through seismic wave data. A seismograph detects minute movements of the Hayward Fault in California and transmits this data via the internet to the installation. The live data stream is visualized on a monitor set in the floor and also converted to low-frequency sounds that reverberate through the enclosed space, echoing unpredictable fluctuations in the Earth's movement. The title links the Japanese term for 'forest sanctuary' with the Latin 'reminder of mortality'. In *Mori*, the immediacy of the link between Earth and visitor invites us to consider the nature of chance, human fragility and geological endurance.

Above

LYNN HERSHMAN LEESON, *AGENT RUBY'S EDREAM PORTAL*, 2002. IRIS PRINT, 20.3 X 25.4 CM (8 X 10 IN)

Left

LYNN HERSHMAN LEESON, *AGENT RUBY MOOD SWING DIAGRAM*, 2002. IRIS PRINT, 76.2 X 101.6 CM (30 X 40 IN)

First brought to virtual life in the film *Teknolust*, which Leeson directed, wrote and co-produced, Agent Ruby is a virtual character whose behaviour is shaped by her interactions with users. Available in a number of versions – film character, website, installation or as downloaded onto a PDA – she communicates with users via speech synthesis and voice recognition, being ultimately able to remember their names and to exhibit a range of moods. Agent Ruby represents the synthetic, 'artificially intelligent' character of the future, who will bridge the gap between real and virtual space.

THE 21ST CENTURY ARRIVED WITH A PANDORA'S BOX OF IDEAS, TOOLS AND TECHNOLOGIES, SUCH AS GENETICS, NANOTECHNOLOGY AND ROBOTICS, THAT WILL AFFECT THE DESTINY OF THE HUMAN RACE. OUR RELATIONSHIP WITH COMPUTER-BASED VIRTUAL LIFE FORMS THAT ARE AUTONOMOUS AND SELF-REPLICATING WILL SHAPE THE FATE OF OUR SPECIES AND BE A CRITICAL ISSUE OF OUR TIME. MY BODY OF WORK ADDRESSES THE SOCIAL CONSTRUCTION OF FEMALE IDENTITY AND RELATED ISSUES OF SOCIAL CONDITIONING, MOST OFTEN THROUGH THE NARRATIVE CONSTRUCT OF AN ALTER EGO OR AGENT.

LYNN HERSHMAN LEESON

I DECIDED TO PUT UP A QUESTIONNAIRE ASKING PEOPLE WHAT KIND OF BODY THEY WOULD LIKE TO HAVE. TO MY SURPRISE, THOUSANDS OF PEOPLE RESPONDED AND WERE ACTUALLY AWAITING THEIR BODIES. THIS LED ME TO CONSIDER THE MEANING OF OUR PERSONIFICATION OF THE WEB, THE RESULTING DATABASES FILLED WITH OUR INFORMATION AND THE NEED TO VISUALIZE OUR VIRTUAL BODIES. I WAS ALSO QUESTIONING THE RHETORIC OF THE TIME, WHICH PROMOTED THE INTERNET AS THE ULTIMATE DEMOCRATIC SPACE.
VICTORIA VESNA

VICTORIA VESNA, *BODIES© INCORPORATED*, 1996. COLLABORATIVE ONLINE PROJECT

Victoria Vesna became involved in net art soon after its emergence. *Bodies© INCorporated* – perhaps one of longest-running net art projects – explores the creation of, and our relationship with, our online alter egos. The website invites participants to assemble a 3D body online: after logging on, the user can design, edit, render and download a virtual body image. Part of the website allows online chat among participants, while another link provides a catalogue of rendered bodies or electronic identities.

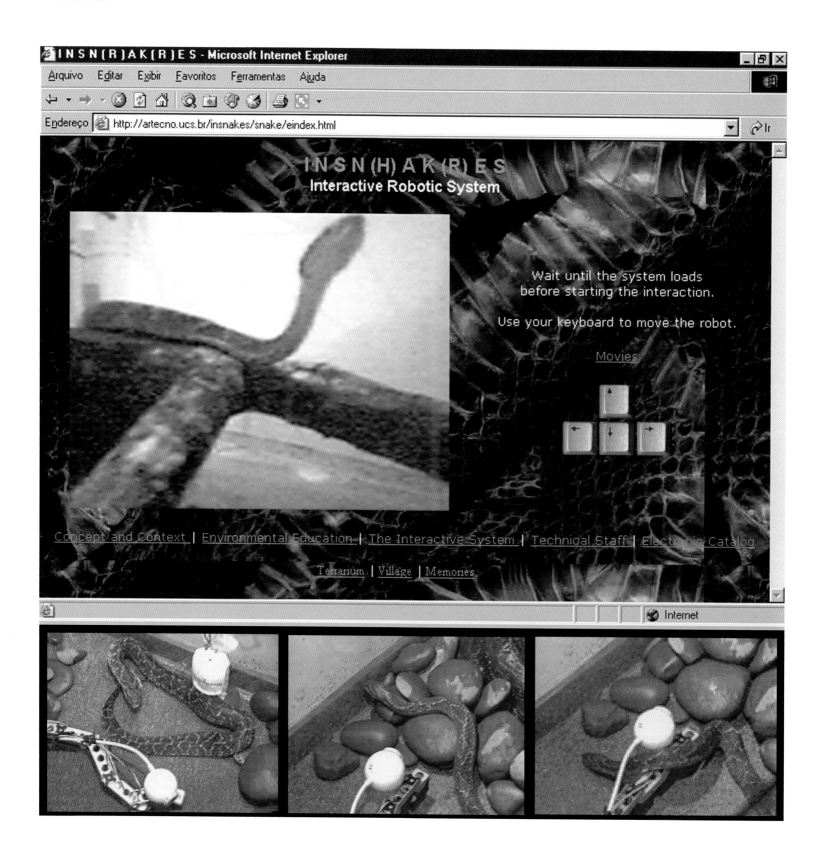

Opposite
DIANA DOMINGUES/ARTECHNO GROUP,
SERPENTARIUM, **2000. NET ART**
This work is an interactive installation accessed
through a website. The interface allows us to control a
robotic snake that broadcasts images and sounds, and
thus to interact in a remote space with living snakes.

Below
DIANA DOMINGUES/ARTECHNO GROUP,
I N S N (H) A K (R) E S, **2000–01.**
CYBERINSTALLATION
People touch the body of a snake to receive a set of
images managed by a neural network, and snakes
appear in a transparent box on the floor.

**LIVING AMONG SNAKES IS PUT AT THE LEVEL OF DREAM AND IMAGINATION.
INTERACTIVE ART ACTS IN A COMPLEX WAY, BECAUSE IT SIMULATES OTHER
KINDS OF WORLDS AND GENERATES NEW FORMS OF LIFE.**
DIANA DOMINGUES

GLYPHITI IS AN IMAGE COMPOSED OF MANY SMALLER 'GLYPHS' THAT CAN BE EDITED EASILY. THE QUALITIES OF THE IMAGE ARE CODETERMINED. AS AUTHOR, I HAVE ESTABLISHED CERTAIN CHARACTERISTICS. THESE INCLUDE THE SIZE AND AVAILABLE COLOURS, WHICH ARE BLACK-AND-WHITE. BUT THE STATE OF EVERY PIXEL CAN BE CHANGED BY THE VISITING ARTIST. CHANGES MADE TO IT ARE SENT TO ALL THOSE WHO ARE CURRENTLY VISITING *GLYPHITI*. THE MARKS EACH PERSON MAKES ARE RECORDED. THE VARIOUS STATES OF THE EVOLVING IMAGE ARE COMBINED AND CAN BE SEEN AS A TIME-LAPSE IMAGE STREAM. IT'S NOT CLEAR EXACTLY WHO OWNS THE COLLABORATIVE IMAGE. FOR MY PART, I ENCOURAGE YOU TO USE IT ANY WAY YOU SEE FIT. I LOOK FORWARD TO SEEING WHAT IMAGES DEVELOP. FINALLY, IF YOU DON'T LIKE THE OPTIONS GIVEN TO YOU, PLEASE REVISE THE SOURCE CODE.
ANDY DECK

ANDY DECK, *GLYPHITI,* 2001– PRESENT.
CUSTOM SOFTWARE, 1024 X 512 PIXELS
Andy Deck's diverse interests include online art-making, political activism, advocating open-source code and collaborative drawing. He maintains two sites, www.andyland.net and www.artcontext.net, both of which contain a variety of art projects, along with links and code for those interested in exploring net art. This image, from the project *Glyphiti*, is a collaborative drawing space created by Deck – effectively an interface in which viewers can modify any part of the drawing they choose. According to the artist, *Glyphiti* has its historical roots in the rock-cut images (glyphs) of the ancient Egyptians and Mayans, as well as being influenced by contemporary digital artist Ken Knowlton.

INSTALLED AT THE CHICAGO CULTURAL CENTER, *THE FILE ROOM* REFERENCES THIS BUILDING'S PAST AS A LIBRARY, A PUBLIC REPOSITORY OF WHAT IS THOUGHT TO BE IMPORTANT. THE INTERACTIVE NATURE OF THE INTERNET (WHICH REMAINS AT THIS MOMENT A FREE SYSTEM FOR DIALOGUE AND INFORMATION) ALLOWS *THE FILE ROOM* TO BECOME A SOCIAL SCULPTURE AS IT MOVES BACK AND FORTH FROM ITS THREE-DIMENSIONAL INSTALLATION TO AN UNKNOWN DIMENSION IN THE NET. WHEN PEOPLE ACTIVATE AND CONTRIBUTE TO THIS ARTWORK, THEY ARE PARTICIPATING IN THE QUESTIONS, CONTRADICTIONS AND LIMITATIONS OF ATTEMPTING TO DEFINE CENSORSHIP. INTERACTIVE TECHNOLOGY IS BEING USED TO ADD NEW POINTS OF VIEW, COMPLETE MISSING INFORMATION, CHALLENGE NOTIONS OF AUTHORSHIP, AND TO REFLECT VOICES AND OPINIONS WHEREVER POSSIBLE.
MUNTADAS

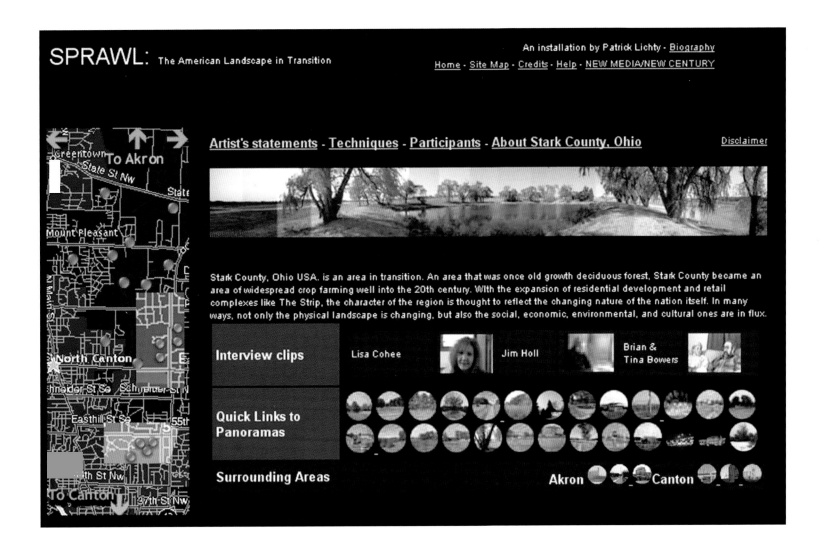

Opposite left
MUNTADAS, *THE FILE ROOM*, 1994. INTERACTIVE MEDIA INSTALLATION, VARIABLE DIMENSIONS
The File Room takes the form of an open archive where participants can either read case histories of censorship or contribute their own examples. It can be accessed online or visited in person. The website includes various definitions of censorship, a searchable archive of cases and a bibliography of anti-censorship resources.

Opposite right
MUNTADAS, *ON TRANSLATION: THE INTERNET PROJECT*, 1996. VARIABLE MEDIA, VARIABLE DIMENSIONS
Part of the *On Translation* series, *The Internet Project* was created for the 1996 Olympics in Atlanta, Georgia. The work took the form of a two-way videoconference between Atlanta and Madrid and highlighted issues surrounding the interpretation of information and the changes of meaning that occur during the process of translation. Muntadas uses the internet to illustrate the cultural differences reflected in language and those occasions when wider global communication – linguistic, social and economic – crosses over into distortion.

Above
PATRICK LICHTY, *SPRAWL*, 2000. ONLINE NEW-MEDIA DOCUMENTARY
Sprawl is an exploration of suburban expansion and resultant changes in social structure using Stark County, Ohio, as a model. Through panoramic photographs, a map interface, video interviews and historical documents, users can develop their own 'picture' of the surrounding community and the landscapes that are forever changed by the area's development. Patrick Lichty received the New Media/New Century Award from the Smithsonian American Art Museum for this work.

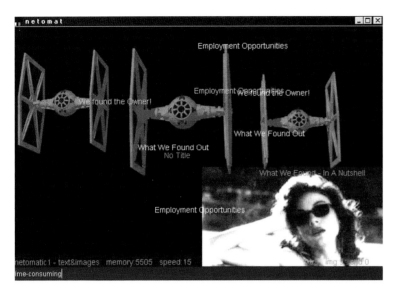

Opposite
MACIEJ WISNIEWSKI, *3 SECONDS IN THE MEMORY OF THE INTERNET*, 2002. NETWORK-BASED MULTI-MEDIA INSTALLATION
For *3 Seconds in the Memory of the Internet*, the artist randomly chose three moments from different decades on the internet using his *netomat™* browser. All the files that had been created or modified at those specific points in time – such as emails, news posts and error files – were then projected as live feeds within a purpose-built installation. The result was visible progression through the sequential digital memory of the internet.

Left
MACIEJ WISNIEWSKI, *NETOMAT™*, 1999. CUSTOM SOFTWARE
Maciej Wisniewski is an artist and programmer who specializes in designing software for the internet. Created to go beyond the usual limitations of web browsers, *netomat™*, a premier example of browser art, offers an alternative approach to sourcing information for the internet. Words or phrases typed in by the viewer prompt the software to find images, text and audio, which are presented as an uninterrupted flow of information within a single virtual space.

Below
ADRIANNE WORTZEL, *DREAM SEQUENCE* FROM *ELIZA REDUX*, 2004. TELEROBOTICS
Working in a wide range of media, including networked robotic installations and performance, Adrianne Wortzel explores concepts of otherness and self-discovery through virtual and physical environments. The robot here responds to text-based human conversation, with the computer playing the role of psychotherapist.

ELIZA REDUX OFFERS INTERACTIVE THEATRE. IT TAKES THE FORM OF ONLINE PSYCHOANALYTIC SESSIONS VIA A WEBSITE, ALLOWING USERS TO INTERACT WITH A ROBOT EQUIPPED WITH AN INTERACTIVE CONVERSATIONAL PROGRAMME IN THE TRADITION OF WEIZENBAUM'S ELIZA.
ADRIANNE WORTZEL

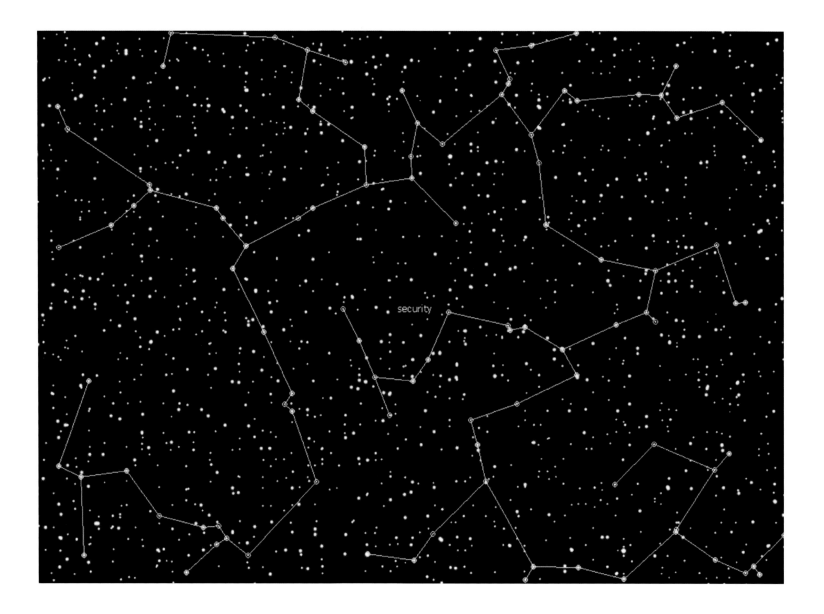

ALEXANDER R. GALLOWAY, MARK TRIBE AND MARTIN WATTENBERG, *STARRYNIGHT*, 1999. ONLINE INTERFACE

StarryNight functions both as net art and as a navigational interface by which one can access the archives of Rhizome.org, the popular online media art website set up by Mark Tribe in 1996. As you scroll across the screen, pieces of text appear, and a click on the corresponding star will reveal an article archived by Rhizome. The stars become brighter with every new click, so viewers are offered a glimpse of the Rhizome community's reading habits, and constellations appear between articles with related topics. As interface art, *StarryNight* exemplifies the possibilities offered by the internet: global collaboration, collection and filtering of information using automated software, and the graphic interpretation of database information.

HOSPITAL ARCHITECTURE IS AN AMALGAM OF ELEMENTS DERIVED FROM RELIGION, THE MILITARY AND THE FACTORY. *LIFE SUPPORT* EXPLORES THIS SYMBOLIC CODING OF SPACE AND ITS UNDERLYING MYTHOLOGIES. IT DRAWS UPON DEPICTIONS OF MEDICAL SPACES IN ADVERTISING, POPULAR CULTURE AND FILM AND THEIR REINTEGRATION INTO OUR VOCABULARY OF SPACE. *LIFE SUPPORT* CREATES A SERIES OF 'ROOMS' BASED ON ARCHETYPAL HOSPITAL SPACES: A CORRIDOR, A WAITING ROOM AND A TREATMENT ROOM. EACH LOCATION IS EXPLORED IN MOVING IMAGES PAIRED WITH SHORT FICTIONS AND ARCHITECTURAL COMMENTARY.
ANNETTE WEINTRAUB

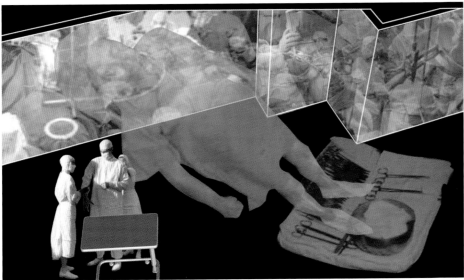

Left
ANNETTE WEINTRAUB, *LIFE SUPPORT (PATIENT ROOM)*, 2003. WEBSITE

Below left
ANNETTE WEINTRAUB, *LIFE SUPPORT (SURGERY)*, 2003. WEBSITE
Annette Weintraub's recent net art piece explores our experiences of space and our psychological relationship with our surroundings. Online architectural constructs form the framework for this creative work. These spaces are hybrids of 2D images and 3D models in which the spatial elements – a 'wire frame' of a room – function as projection screens and as containers for audio narratives. Weintraub used Macromedia Flash software in this work to create several layers of images, animation, text and audio.

I WORK WITH TECHNOLOGY BECAUSE IT IS IMPOSSIBLE NOT TO. TECHNOLOGY IS ONE OF THE INEVITABLE LANGUAGES OF GLOBALIZATION. I LIKE CALLING IT A LANGUAGE BECAUSE THIS CONVEYS TWO ATTRIBUTES THAT ARE SIGNIFICANT. FIRSTLY, TECHNOLOGY IS INSEPARABLE FROM CONTEMPORARY IDENTITY – THERE IS NO SUCH THING AS 'WHAT WE WERE LIKE BEFORE TECHNOLOGY' – AND SECONDLY, IT IS NOT SOMETHING THAT HAS BEEN INVENTED OR ENGINEERED, BUT RATHER IT HAS EVOLVED THROUGH CONSTANTLY CHANGING SOCIAL, ECONOMIC, PHYSICAL AND POLITICAL FORCES. I THINK ARTISTS USE TECHNOLOGY EXPLICITLY AS A WAY TO UNDERSTAND AND CRITICIZE SOME OF THE PARADOXES OF OUR CULTURE.
RAFAEL LOZANO-HEMMER

RAFAEL LOZANO-HEMMER, *VECTORIAL ELEVATION: RELATIONAL ARCHITECTURE 4,* **1999–2004. ONLINE INTERFACE AND INSTALLATION**
Mexican–Canadian artist Rafael Lozano-Hemmer specializes in large-scale interactive installations that allow local or remote participants to transform buildings or urban landscapes through sensors, networks, robots and audiovisual technologies. This particular work was initially created for the millennium celebrations at Zócalo Square in Mexico City. Over 800,000 people from 89 countries visited the website during a two-week period in order to manipulate the 18 robotic searchlights, and the light sculptures could be seen from a ten-mile radius. The project subsequently travelled to various sites in Europe.

THE FUTURE OF DIGITAL ART

When speculating about the future of digital art, one must stand at a crossroads and look down two avenues: art and technology. Artists of the future will have never known a world without computers, and creating art with digital tools and media will not be perceived as something unusual. Contemporary art will continue to evolve, quietly incorporating new technologies as part of its development, and will continue to integrate with popular culture as well as with daily life. The revolution in global communication that the internet has provided will also bring greater multi-cultural interaction and understanding.

Preservation and archiving

Public awareness and interest in digital art is growing – museums, galleries and contemporary art centres are now showing new media artworks. Museums have also begun to address the technological difficulties in exhibiting and preserving digital works, and the number of curators involved with this art form is constantly growing. The need to establish permanence for these artworks is fuelling the technological advancements required to solve these issues. Mark Tribe, founder of Rhizome.org, has described four methods for the preservation of digital art: documentation (screen grabs, artist diagrams, installation instructions and statements), migration (updating work to accommodate newer technology and file formats), emulation (running projects through software that allows them to work on newer hardware), and recreation (remaking the artwork for a new technical environment).

Organizations are now involved with archiving new media: one example is the Variable Media Network (www.variablemedia.net), which grew out of the Solomon R. Guggenheim Museum's efforts to preserve its collection of conceptual, minimalist and video art. This affiliation of museums, art centres, foundations and artists' groups is involved in developing strategies, methods and standards for the preservation of contemporary art.

Trends in technological advancement

A looking glass that could see the future of technology would indeed be a very valuable one. The stages of maturation of various technologies give us a glimpse at where the future of digital technologies are heading. For example, Microsoft Word is a fully mature technology for writing, with the functionality needed already in the software: editing, spelling and grammar checks, and even multilingual dictionaries. Digital imaging has also become a mature technology, with Photoshop offering precise control over image creation and manipulation. Digital audio is another widespread technology: high-quality recording, editing and playback software are well within the capabilities of the average desktop computer today.

The MP3 and other digital audio formats have changed how music is disseminated and downloaded, and demonstrate how technology can significantly alter media distribution systems. Napster revolutionized the recording industry, which has now adopted online sales through websites such as Apple's iTunes. Digital video is rapidly becoming a mature technology and is using these same systems. The Apple iPod is now photo and video capable. Image resolution will continue to increase, as proved by the development of high-definition television (HDTV) and DVDs. Even affordable DVD authoring software is now readily available. While non-linear video editing systems such as Avid have been industry standards for years, Apple Final Cut Pro and Adobe Premiere Pro are rapidly developing the possibilities available to artists, offering broadcast-quality desktop editing.

Data storage, bandwidth and interactivity

To begin, we will continue to see data being stored and delivered in better quality formats. There are three underlying factors to consider: data storage, bandwidth and interactivity. Storage capacity and bandwidth capabilities will continue to increase. Some of this technology is already in place, such as cable modems and DSL. The Internet2, Access Grid and National LambdaRail are research networks developing software and technologies for ultra-high speed data transmission and multiple simultaneous streams of video and audio. It is clear from recent Hollywood films that new technologies have blurred the boundaries between what is 'real' and 'artificial'. When watching early special effects, we willingly suspended our disbelief to enjoy the film. Today, that separation no longer exists. The same is true with audio, as surround-sound technologies and ever higher sample rates and bit depths have made the creation of a believable immersive sound environment commonplace. Future generations will see high-definition video and multi-channel surround-sound as the de facto standard. Three-dimensional television, projection and immersive environments will become the next media frontier.

Finally, what emerging technologies will be important to society, as well as to creative expression? Software development is critical to future technological development. Compression technologies, fibre optics and more advanced wireless networks need to be developed to allow for high-definition full-frame video and multi-channel surround-sound for home users and mobile users, as well as for the benefit of public institutions such as museums and galleries.

Gaming and virtual reality

We need only look to the video game industry as an example of the fertile creative territories yet to be explored. Over the past ten years, video games have been at the cutting edge of technology. Video games have surpassed feature films in terms of revenue and a new genre of three-dimensional computer animated feature films has emerged. 'Gaming machines' are the fastest and best-equipped personal computers, since the creation of real-time environments requires tremendous computing power. If we speculate about the potential increases in computing power and the development of artificial intelligence in video games, and then combine these initiatives with the feature film industry, we can begin to imagine a completely new type of virtual environment.

Although there have been many virtual works created with immersive systems, it is through future technology that these environments will be truly believable and of greater interest to both artists and participants. For example, by merging video game technology with feature film quality three-dimensional animation, one could push the 'play' button and view a film from the director's viewpoint or from the different perspectives of any character in the environment. In addition, since these characters are programmed with artificial intelligence, viewers could also create their own movies by moving through the environment while recording the experience. This union of interactivity and artificial intelligence technologies will expand our options for creating and experiencing media.

Wireless and beyond

Wireless technology will also play a very important role in the arts. This is already apparent in the case of mobile phones and PDAs, which began as voice-only devices and have evolved into camera phones with internet capabilities. Videophones will soon be widely available. Many technologists have proclaimed wireless technology as the future 'promised land'. Freed from the restraints of location, it will enable art and media to be experienced literally anywhere. This is not to suggest that galleries and museums will diminish in their importance, but rather handheld and other portable devices will add a new dimension to the art experience, whether outside or inside the art space. The challenge for artists will be to create works that can transcend different venues and media, and in so doing reach a larger audience.

Undoubtedly, new interfaces will emerge as cutting-edge technology becomes more ubiquitous. The paradigm of the keyboard, monitor and mouse may remain, but new technologies will augment and perhaps replace them. Haptic interfaces are being developed to heighten the tactile experience. The combination of three-dimensional imagery, interfaces, voice recognition and position sensors will eventually allow people to converse with someone in a remote global location as if they were in the same room. While this may sound like science fiction, the tools of creative expression have never been more powerful, and, in many ways, the future of art has never looked brighter.

A TIMELINE OF DIGITAL ART AND TECHNOLOGY

PRE-DIGITAL PRECEDENTS

1450 Gutenberg invents movable type and the printing press.

1868 The typewriter is designed by Christopher Sholes and built by Remington in 1874.

1876 The telephone is invented by Alexander Graham Bell.

1877 Thomas Edison develops the phonograph.

1887 Motion picture camera patented by Thomas Edison.

1888 Eadweard Muybridge publishes his series of photographs, *Studies of Animal Locomotion*.

1895 Louis and Auguste Lumière produce two of the earliest motion pictures, *Workers Leaving the Lumière Factory in Lyon* and *A Trip to the Moon* in 1902.

1901 Guglielmo Marconi transmits Morse code across the Atlantic Ocean and ushers in the age of radio.

1920 Léon Theremin creates an electronic musical instrument based on an oscillating circuit, the Theremin, which is controlled by hand gestures.

1927 The first television picture is transmitted by Philo Farnsworth.

1931 The first stereo recordings are made.

1939 Television debuts at the New York World's Fair.

1939– John Cage creates *Imaginary Landscapes*,
1952 a series of early electronic music works and performances.

THE DIGITAL AGE

1946 ENIAC, one of the first computers, is built using 18,000 vacuum tubes.

1950s SAGE Air Defense computers convert radar signals into computer graphic images. The light pen is introduced.

1950 Ben Laposky uses oscilloscopes to display waveform patterns that are photographed and exhibited.

1963 American Standard Code for Information Interchange (ASCII) is adopted as a standard for computer text.

1963 Mellotron instrument is invented, which uses tape loops to create its sound.

1963 First computer graphics software is created by Ivan Sutherland at MIT called Sketchpad.

1963 Lapis film is produced by John Whitney, Sr.

1963 Nam Jun Paik exhibits *Random Access*, using strips of magnetic tape and tape heads that gallery attendees swipe to produce sounds.

1964 Stan Vanderbeek and Ken Knowlton produce the computer-animated film, *Poem Field*.

1965 First computer art exhibition at the Technische Hochschule in Stuttgart, Germany.

1965 Early computer art exhibitions at the Technische Hochschule in Stuttgart, Germany and the Howard Wise Gallery in New York.

1965 Stereo computer animations are created by A. Michael Noll and Bela Julesz at Bell Labs in New Jersey.

1966 Billy Klüver starts Experiments in Art and Technology (EAT).

1966 Charles A. Csuri produces the computer-animated film, *Hummingbird*, which is later purchased by MoMA.

1968 The mouse is invented by Douglas Englebart.

1968 John Whitney, Sr. creates the computer-animated film, *Permutations*.

1968 One of the first computer art exhibitions, 'Cybernetic Serendipity: the Computer and the Arts' held at the Institute of Contemporary Arts (ICA) in London.

1968 'Machine As Seen at the End of the Mechanical Age' exhibition is held at the Museum of Modern Art in New York.

1968 *Leonardo* journal is first published in Paris by founder Frank J. Malina.

1969 Myron Kreuger develops one of the first prototypes of virtual reality.

1969 ARPANET is set up by the United States Department of Defense.

1969 The first frame buffer is developed by Bell Labs, which allows the storage of a single digital image.

1969 The Studio for Electro-Instrumental Music (STEIM) is established in Amsterdam.

1970 Xerox established the Palo Alto Research Center (PARC) at Stanford University.

1970 The first high definition colour computer graphic workstation, Genigraphics, is created by General Electric.

1970 *Expanded Cinema*, written by Gene Youngblood is published.

1973 ACM SIGGRAPH, the special interest group in graphics established.

1974 *Hunger*, an early computer animated film by Peter Foldes is produced at the National Film Board of Canada.

1975 Benoit Mandelbrot develops fractals at IBM.

1976 Franklin Furnace is founded by Martha Wilson in New York.

1977 The Apple II computer becomes the first personal computer with colour graphics.

1977 Institut de Recherche et Coordination Acoustique/Musique (IRCAM) is established in France.

1977 *Satellite Arts Project* by Kit Galloway and Sherrie Rabinowitz.

1979 The Fairlight Computer Musical Instrument CMI is invented. It is the first digital music synthesizer.

1979 The Modulator/Demodulator or MODEM is invented, allowing digital signals to travel over analogue phone lines.

1979 Ars Electronica Festival started in Linz, Austria.

1979 *Lorna*, one of the first videodisks by an artist created by Lynn Hershman Leeson.

1980 The MIT Media Laboratory is founded by Nicholas Negroponte.

1981 IBM releases their first PC computer.

1982 *The World in 24 Hours*, one of the first global telecommunications art events, is produced by Robert Adrian.

1982 Adobe Systems is founded.

1982 International Society for the Arts, Sciences and Technology (Leonardo/ISAST) is founded by Roger F. Malina.

1983 The compact disk (CD) is introduced.

1983 *Growth*, the first in a series of computer animations is created by Yoichiro Kawaguchi.

1984 Musical Instrument Digital Interface (MIDI) is established, which enables digital synthesizers from different manufacturers to communicate with each other.

1984 The first Macintosh computer is released.

1984 Kit Galloway and Sherrie Rabinowitz co-found the Electronic Cafe.

1985 AT&T develops the TARGA 16 graphic card, allowing for 16-bit images and 32,000 colours.

1986 DAT or digital audio tape is introduced by Sony/Phillips.

1986 Nicolas Schöffer receives the Frank J. Malina Lifetime Achievement Award.

1986 *Very Nervous System* created by David Rokeby.

1987 First Master of Fine Arts degree programme in Computer Art in the United States started at the School of Visual Arts in New York.

1987 Prix Ars Electronic is established to recognize significant achievements in cyberarts.

1988 The Renderman shading language is released by Pixar and received a US patent.

1988 Australian Network for Art and Technology (ANAT) is established.

1988 Art Science Collaborations Inc. (ASCI) is founded by Cynthia Pannucci to support technology-based art.

1989 Jeffrey Shaw creates an interactive work, *The Legible City*.

1990 Karl Sims produces *Panspermia*, one of the first computer animations to be produced by a single individual.

1990 Kenneth Snelson creates some of the first virtual sculptures using 3D software.

1991 William Latham at IBM UK produces the computer animation, *Mutations*.

1991 James F. Blinn is named a MacArthur Fellow for his pioneering work in computer animation.

1991 The MP3 digital audio compression format is developed at the Fraunhofer Institute, Germany.

1991 The Thing, a bulletin board service focusing on contemporary art and cultural theory is launched in New York.

1992 HyperText Markup Language (HTML) is developed for the internet, paving the way for the World Wide Web.

1993 The first New York Digital Salon is held at the Art Directors Club in New York.

1993 Mosaic, the first graphical web browser is released.

1993 Karl Sims creates a series of software-based works, *Genetic Images*

1994 The Netscape browser is introduced.

1994 *A-Volve*, the interactive real-time environment, is created by Christa Sommerer and Laurent Mignonneau.

1994 Electronic Music Foundation established by Joel Chadabe.

1995 RealAudio standard is introduced which allows for streaming data over the internet. RealVideo is introduced shortly after.

1995 Nettime founded to promote international networked discourse.

1995 *Osmose*, an immersive interactive virtual reality environment is created by Char Davies.

1996 Benjamin Weil, Vivian Selbo and Andrea Scott found äda'web, a multi-artist net art project.

1996 DVD video is introduced.

1996 Eyebeam is founded by John S. Johnson in New York.

1996 Rhizome.org founded to provide a platform for the global new media community.

1996 Postmasters Gallery in New York starts promoting digital art with the exhibition 'Can You Digit?'

1997 MP3.com is founded by Michael Robertson.

1997 'Digital Atelier: A Printmaking Studio for the 21st Century' at the Smithsonian Museum of American Art is organized by Dorothy Simpson Krause.

1997 Steve Dietz establishes Gallery 9, a net art gallery at the Walker Art Center.

1998 Char Davies creates the 3D virtual reality immersive environment *Ephémère*.

1998 Karl Sims is named a MacArthur Fellow in digital art and computer science.

1999 Paul Debevec uses image-based rendering to produce the animation, *Fiat Lux*.

1999 The first recordable CD-ROM is developed by Sony and Phillips.

1999 Vectorial Elevation by Rafael Lozano-Hemmer allows internet users to control a light

installation in Mexico City.

1999 *Glasbead*, an interactive music work, is created by John Klima.

2000 Jodi creates www.jodi.org, one of best-known net art websites.

2000 DVD becomes the best-selling technology ever.

2000 The Digital Art Museum (DAM) in Berlin becomes an online digital art museum.

2001 San Francisco MoMA exhibits '010101: Art in Technological Times'.

2001 The Whitney Museum of American Art presents the 'BitStreams' and 'Data Dynamics' exhibitions.

2001 Brooklyn Museum opens the 'Digital Printmaking' exhibition.

2001 DA2, digital arts development agency is established in the UK.

2001 Alexander R. Galloway and the Radical Software Group create Carnivore software.

2001 Erwin Redl's *Matrix IV* is exhibited at the Whitney Museum in New York.

2001 *Pockets Full of Memories* installation is created by George Legrady.

2001 Martin Wattenberg and Marek Walczak create the net art piece, *The Apartment*.

2001 'Game Show' exhibition at the Massachusetts Museum of Contemporary Art.

2001 Apple Computer, Inc. releases the iPod digital music player.

2001 Bitforms Gallery, featuring digital art, opens in New York.

2002 DigiArts website is added to the UNESCO Knowledge Portal.

2002 Whitney Museum of American Art portal to net art and digital art, ARTPORT, is launched.

2002 'INSTALL.EXE', the first United States solo exhibition by Jodi at Eyebeam.

2003 New York Digital Salon celebrates its 10th anniversary with 'VECTORS: Digital Art of Our Time exhibition at the World Financial Center in New York City'.

2003 ACM SIGGRAPH Art Gallery celebrates its 30th anniversary.

2003 Jeremy Gardiner wins the Peterborough Art Prize for *Purbeck Light Years*.

2003 'NANO' exhibition by Victoria Vesna, James Gimzewski and others begins at Los Angeles County Museum of Art.

2004 First Beijing International New Media Arts Exhibition and Symposium.

2004 Chris Landreth wins the Academy Award for Best Animated Short Film with *Ryan*.

2004 *Vectorial Elevation* by Rafael Lozano-Hemmer is installed in Dublin, Ireland.

2005 Vera Molnar receives the first lifetime achievement d.velop digital art award (ddaa).

2005 The Boston Cyberarts Festival celebrates the use of technology in the arts.

2006 Inter-Society for Electronic Arts (ISEA) Pacific Rim New Media Summit is held.

2006 New York Digital Salon debuts the Abstract Visual Music website, exhibition and events.

2006 NODE.London, media art festival begins.

GLOSSARY

ALGORITHM

An algorithm is a set of instructions (mathematical and/or text) that defines a procedure or solution to a problem in a finite number of steps. Algorithms become computer programmes when written in a programming language.

ANALOGUE

The encoding of signals and data that is continuously variable, such as voltage and frequency. Older magnetic tapes for audio and video recordings were produced through the analogue process rather than in binary form. Digital devices encode information in discrete units through the binary system of zeros and ones.

ARCHIVAL

Archival is a descriptor that refers to the degree of permanence of materials and the length of time an artwork will last. Archival papers are acid free and do not change colour with age. The advent of digital photography has brought archival papers and pigments to desktop printers.

ARTIFICIAL INTELLIGENCE (AI)

The use of computers and software for the simulation of thought processes and human behaviour. Speech recognition, language processing, problem solving, computer vision and robotics are examples.

ARTIFICIAL LIFE (A-LIFE)

The study of artificial life strives to model and duplicate living biological systems and structures through computer systems and algorithms. Cellular automata and virtual pets are examples.

BANDWIDTH

Bandwidth refers to data transmission capacity, which is measured in bits per second (bps). 56K dial-up is capable of transmitting 56,000 bits of data per second; DSL and cable modems are much faster; T1 and T3 lines transmit at 1.544 and 44.7 megabits per second, respectively.

BAUHAUS

Founded in 1919, the Bauhaus School promoted the integration of the fine arts and design with the study of craft, primarily in architecture, painting and sculpture. Initially headed by Walter Gropius, with a faculty that included Josef Albers, Wassily Kandinsky, Paul Klee and László Moholy-Nagy, the Bauhaus stressed functionalism, emphasizing that art did not only reflect a society, but could also have an impact upon it.

BIT, BYTE

In the digital realm, all information is converted into a binary system comprised of zeros and ones. A bit (a contraction of the words 'binary' and 'digit') is a single digital unit – a zero or a one. A byte is a group of eight bits. Bits per second (bps) is the measurement used to define the rate at which a digital signal is transmitted.

BITMAP

A graphic representation comprised of an array of rows and columns of dots or pixels. For black-and-white systems, one bit represents one black or white pixel on the screen. For colours and shades of grey, each pixel requires more than one bit of data to define the colour. The density of the dots (resolution) determines the quality and detail of the image or file. In general, resolution is expressed in dots per inch (dpi) for printing or by the number of rows and columns (i.e. 1024 x 768) for screen images.

COMPUTER-AIDED DESIGN (CAD)

The use of computers for design, particularly in architecture, interior design and manufacturing. CAD systems have replaced many manual tasks because of their mathematical precision and ability to make quick changes. CAD systems combined with manufacturing are referred to as CAD/CAM, computer-aided design and manufacturing.

CONCEPTUAL ART

Also known as 'idea art', the conceptual art movement began in the 1960s and extended to the late 1970s. Its tenet embodies the notion that the primary purpose or function of an artwork is to convey its idea or concept; to that end, the physical creation is almost superfluous to the work. Some conceptual artworks are complete when the artist has detailed the piece through text, never fabricating it in a tangible form.

CONSTRUCTIVISM

Emerging from Russia in the 1920s, Constructivism is characterized as an art movement involved with the 'culture of materials', a phrase coined by Vladimir Tatlin, one of its main proponents. A principle of Constructivism was to move away from easel art to develop the idea of artist/engineer by expanding the artist's repertoire beyond painting, drawing and sculpture.

CYBERNETICS

The science and study of communication between humans and machines, control systems and automata. The relationships between living and non-living self-regulating systems are examples of cybernetic research.

CYBERSPACE

First defined in *Neuromancer* by William Gibson, the term refers to navigable information space; cyberspace is also used in reference to virtual reality spaces and the internet.

DADA

This early 20th-century international art movement was born from protest of the First World War, conservative social mores and traditional art forms. Dada artists produced works that were both nihilistic and playful, by creating art using unconventional methods. Many Dada artists were later involved with Surrealism. Dada was influential to several art movements, including Fluxus. Anti-Art is steeped in the Dadaist tradition – rejecting traditional art forms and conventional art theory.

DATABASE

A collection of data records that is organized and accessed through various descriptors and keywords. Database software provides an interface through which one can input, view, sort and manipulate the information. For example, a database of an address book can be searched by name, area code, post or zip code, etc. MySQL and PHP are popular database programming languages for the internet. FileMaker Pro can store photographs and text and is searchable by a defined descriptor.

DIGITIZE

The process of converting analogue media – drawings, photographs, video, sound – into digital form (data). Various file formats exist for different types of medio.

FLUXUS

Begun in the early 1960s, Fluxus was an avant-garde art movement that revelled in spontaneity and humour, striving to blend previously distinct disciplines such as visual art, music and literature.

Named after its Latin roots for 'flow' and 'change' Fluxus heralded artistic exploration and activism, and was known for staging happenings, particularly performance art and street theatre, which involved public participation.

FUTURISM
Originating in Italy circa 1910, Futurist artworks expressed the dynamism and kinetic rhythms of society at the dawn of the machine age. Rejecting the past, these artists were enthused by the innovations, movement and speed of the modern world.

GICLÉE
Taken from the French *gicler* – 'to spray' or 'to squirt' – giclée has become an industry moniker that refers to high quality, digitally produced inkjet prints. Giclée is widely used for fine art printmaking and can print on archival paper, canvas and film.

GLOBAL POSITIONING SYSTEM (GPS)
Designed and controlled by the United States Department of Defense, this navigation system is comprised of satellites, computers and receivers that transmit continuous radio signals as the satellites orbit the earth. These signals provide exact position, velocity and time information to users. OnStar is an example of a GPS system that assists drivers. Artists have created site-specific works using GPS-capable mobile phones.

GRAPHICAL USER INTERFACE (GUI)
A way of communicating with a computer using icons, pictures, windows and menus. Operating systems such as Microsoft Windows and Apple OS X are based on the graphical user interface. GUIs that are application or hardware specific include ATM touchscreens, mobile phones and games.

HAPTIC INTERFACE DEVICE
Video game controllers and VR data gloves that sense body movement are haptic (or touch related) interfaces. These devices incorporate various features, including pressure sensitivity, mechanical feedback and 3D position information. For example, using a video game controller steering wheel with built-in feedback.

IMMERSIVE EXPERIENCE
The act of entering and navigating through a synthetic 3D environment (digital or otherwise). Most commonly associated with virtual reality systems that use a head-mounted display and data glove, many installation artworks also incorporate immersive properties.

INTERACTIVE MUSIC
Music in which the participant controls what is heard. This can range from a simple interface where the music mix is altered, to something as sophisticated as *Very Nervous System* by David Rokeby where sounds are mapped to a video image and the slightest body movement creates music and sound.

INTERACTIVITY
A dialogue between the viewer and the art. The experience is active and requires viewer participation as opposed to passive activities, such as listening to music or watching video.

INTERFACE
The point of contact, communication and control between the user and the computer or software programme.

META-FORMS, POLYFORMS
Data files that can be output in multiple forms, such as a print, physical sculpture, or QuickTime VR file.

MUSICAL INSTRUMENT DIGITAL INTERFACE (MIDI)
MIDI is a standard for communication between electronic musical instruments and computers. It has both a hardware specification and a software protocol. MIDI can also be used for other machine control routines, i.e. DVD players.

NANOTECHNOLOGY
Technology that exists on an atomic or molecular level. Used to build microscopic electronic circuits and devices, nanotechnology will enable future developments in computer storage, semiconductors and other devices requiring miniaturization.

OUTSIDER ART
Defined in its most inclusive form, outsider art refers to artworks created by people with no formal art training and/or by individuals not involved in the traditional art establishment.

PROGRAMMING LANGUAGES, SCRIPTING LANGUAGES
A programme is a set of instructions that determines how a computer performs a particular task. A scripting language contains many pre-programmed routines and functions and is a subset of a programming language.

RAPID PROTOTYPING
Technologies that can fabricate physical models from 3D data files. Designers can create objects from their designs far more quickly and inexpensively with rapid prototyping than by most traditional methods.

SOURCE CODE, OPEN SOURCE
Written by the programmer, source code is an editable computer programme. It is generally compiled into an application or executable file. Many programmers and companies protect their source code, while others choose an open source model. With open source the code is freely available and distributed. Linux is an example of an open source operating system.

TELE-
A descriptor for the control of various artworks, processes and devices from a distance, i.e. telerobotics.

TELECOMMUNICATIONS
A general term for the exchange of information over long distances via the airwaves, networks, or telephones.

VERSIONING
Used to describe updated and modified software, versioning also applies to installation art that changes in configuration with each exhibition.

VIRTUAL SCULPTURE
Sculpture created within the computer or cyberspace that is generally achieved with 3D modelling software. The virtual environment allows the sculptor to bypass concerns such as weight, gravity and other physical constraints.

VISUAL MUSIC
The synchronization of visual and musical components in a work of art – commonly a video, animation, or new media performance. Other types of visual music include painting, sculpture and dance.

FURTHER READING

The books, journals, essays and exhibition catalogues that follow are intended to provide the reader with additional research materials, including works on theory, history, practice and the different types of digital art. Many contain bibliographies, URLs and additional resources for the reader.

ACM SIGGRAPH, Special Interest Group in Graphics, *Visual Proceedings* (and other publications.

Ars Electronica, CyberArts (catalogues of conferences and awards)

Ascott, Roy and Edward A. Shanken (ed.), *Telematic Embrace: Visionary Theories of Art, Technology and Consciousness* (Berkeley: University of California Press, 2003)

Baumgartel, Tilman, *net.art 2.0: New Materials Towards Net Art* (Germany: Verlag Moderne Kunst Nurnberg, 2001)

Benedikt, Michael (ed.), *Cyberspace, First Steps* (Cambridge, Mass.: MIT Press, 1991)

Benjamin, Walter, 'The Work of Art in the Age of Mechanical Reproduction', in Arendt, H. (ed.), *Illumination* (New York: Schocken Books, 1968)

Burnham, Jack, *Beyond Modern Sculpture: The Effects of Science and Technology on the Sculpture of This Century* (New York: George Braziller, 1968)

Chadabe, Joel, *Electric Sound: The Past and Promise of Electronic Music* (Upper Saddle River: Prentice Hall, 1997)

Coleman, A. D., *The Digital Evolution* (New York: Nazraeli Press, 1998)

Druckery, Timothy (ed.), *Ars Electronica: Facing the Future* (Cambridge, Mass.: MIT Press, 1999)

Druckery, Timothy (ed.), *Electronic Culture: Technology and Visual Representation* (New York: Aperture, 1997)

Gere, Charlie, *Digital Culture* (London: Reaktion Books Ltd, 2002)

Goldberg, Ken (ed.), *The Robot in the Garden: Telerobotics and Telepistemology in the Age of the Internet* (Cambridge, Mass.: MIT Press, 2001)

Goldberg, RoseLee, *Performance Art* (London: Thames & Hudson, 2001)

Goodman, Cynthia, *Digital Visions: Computers and Art* (New York: Harry N. Abrams, Inc., 1987)

Grau, Oliver, *Virtual Art: From Illusion to Immersion* (Cambridge, Mass.: MIT Press, 2003)

Greene, Rachel, *Internet Art* (London: Thames & Hudson, 2004)

Hall, Doug and Jo Fifer, Sally (eds), *Illuminating Video: An Essential Guide to Video Art* (New York: Aperture, 1990)

Johnson, Steven, *Interface Culture* (New York: Basic Books, 1999)

Kandinsky, Wassily, *Concerning the Spiritual in Art* (New York: Dover Publications, Inc., 1977)

Leeson, Lynn Hershman, *Clicking In: Hot Links To a Digital Culture* (Washington: Bay Press, 1996)

Leonardo: Journal of the International Society for the Arts, Sciences and Technology (Cambridge, Mass.: MIT Press)

Lovejoy, Margot, *Digital Currents: Art in the Electronic Age* (New York and London: Routledge, 2004)

Lunenfeld, Peter (ed.), *The Digital Dialectic: New Essays on New Media* (Cambridge, Mass.: MIT Press, 2000)

Maeda, John, *Maeda @ Media* (London: Thames & Hudson, 2000)

Malina, Frank J. (ed.), *Kinetic Art: Theory and Practice* (New York: Dover Publications, Inc., 1974)

Malloy, Judy (ed.), *Women, Art and Technology* (Cambridge, Mass.: MIT Press, 2003)

Manovich, Lev, *The Language of New Media*, (Cambridge, Mass.: MIT Press, 2002)

Mattis, Olivia et al., *Visual Music: Synaesthesia in Art and Music Since 1900*, (London: Thames & Hudson, 2005)

McLuhan, Marshall and Powers, Bruce, *The Global Village: Transformations in World Life and Media in the 21st Century* (New York: Oxford University Press, 1989)

Moser, Mary Anne and MacLeod, Douglas (eds), *Immersed in Technology: Art and Virtual Environments* (Cambridge, Mass.: MIT Press, 1995)

Packer, Randall and Jordan, Ken (eds), *Multimedia: From Wagner to Virtual Reality* (New York: W. W. Norton & Company, Inc., 2001)

Paul, Christiane, *Digital Art* (London: Thames & Hudson, 2003)

Popper, Frank, *Art of the Electronic Age* (London: Thames & Hudson, 1993)

Rush, Michael, *New Media in Art* (London: Thames & Hudson, second edition, 2005)

Shaw, Jeffrey and Weibel, Peter (eds), *Future Cinema: The Cinematic Imaginary After Film* (Cambridge, Mass.: MIT Press, 2003)

Sommerer, Christa and Mignonneau, Laurent (eds), *Art @ Science* (New York: Springer, 1998)

Spiller, Neil (ed.), *Cyber_Reader: Critical Writings for the Digital Era* (New York: Phaidon, 2002)

Wands, Bruce, *Digital Creativity: Techniques for Digital Media and the Internet* (New York: John Wiley & Sons, Inc., 2002)

Wardrip-Fruin, Noah and Montfort, Nick (eds), *The New Media Reader* (Cambridge, Mass.: MIT Press, 2003)

Weibel, Peter and Druckrey, Timothy (eds), *net_condition: Art and Global Media* (Cambridge, Mass.: MIT Press, 2001)

Wilson, Stephen, *Information Arts: Intersections of Art, Science and Technology* (Cambridge, Mass.: MIT Press, 2002)

Woolman, Matt, *Sonic Graphics: Seeing Sound* (London: Thames & Hudson, 2002)

Youngblood, Gene, *Expanded Cinema* (New York: E. P. Dutton and Co., 1970)

Zielinski, S. *Deep Time of the Media: Toward an Archaeology of Hearing and Seeing by Technical Means* (Cambridge, Mass.: MIT Press, 2006)

DIGITAL ART RESOURCES

This list provides a research tool to further learn about international digital art. An online list is available on the Thames & Hudson website for this book: http://www.thamesandhudson.com/en/1/0500238170.mxs

Acoustic Space Lab
http://acoustic.space.re-lab.net/labAustralian
Network for Art and Technology (ANAT)
http://www.anat.org.au
Ars Electronica
http://aec.at
Art & Science Collaborations, Inc. (ASCI)
http://www.asci.org
Artnetweb
http://www.artnetweb.com
Artport, Whitney Museum of American Art Portal to Net Art
http://artport.whitney.org
Banff New Media Institute
http://www.banffcentre.ca/bnmi/programs
Bitforms
http://www.bitforms.com
Boston Cyberarts Gallery
http://gallery.bostoncyberarts.org
C3 Center for Culture and Communication
http://www.c3.hu
CACHe
http://www.bbk.ac.uk/hosted/cache
Centre Pompidou Net Art
http://www.centrepompidou.fr/netart
Curatorial Resource for upstart Media Bliss (CRUMB)
http://www.newmedia.sunderland.ac.uk/crumb
Database of Virtual Art
http://www.virtualart.at
Dutch Electronic Art Festival (DEAF)
http://www.v2.nl.DEAF
DIA Center for the Arts Web Projects
http://www.diacenter.org/webproj/index.html
Digital Art Museum (DAM)
http://www.dam.org
Electronic Arts Intermix
http://www.eai.org/eai
Electronic Music Foundation
http://www.emf.org
Engine 27
http://www.engine27.org
Experimental Television Center

http://www.experimentaltvcenter.org
Eyebeam Atelier
http://www.eyebeam.org
fineArt forum
http://www.msstate.edu/Fineart_Online/home.html
Fondation Daniel Langlois
http://www.fondation-langlois.org
Foundation for Art and Creative Technology (FACT)
http://www.fact.co.uk
Franklin Furnace
http://www.franklinfurnace.org
Harvestworks Media Arts Center
http://www.harvestworks.org
Intercommunication Center Online (ICC Center)
http://www.ntticc.or.jp
Inter-Society for the Electronic Arts (ISEA)
http://www.isea-web.org
IRCAM
http://www.ircam.fr
Java Museum
http://www.nmartproject.net
The Kitchen
http://www.thekitchen.org
Leonardo/International Society for the Arts, Sciences and Technology
http://mitpress.mit.edu
Location 1
http://www.location1.org
Ljubljana Digital Media Lab
http://www.ljudmila.org
Multimedia Art Research Centres and Electronic Laboratories (MARCEL)
http://www.mmmarcel.org
Medi@terra
http://www.mediaterra.org
Net Art Review
http://www.netartreview.net
Nettime
http://www.nettime.org
Netzspannung Internet Media Laboratory
http://netzspannung.org

New Media Beijing
http://www.newmediabeijing.org
New Media Scotland
http://www.mediascot.org
New York Digital Salon
http://www.nydigitalsalon.org
Postmasters Gallery
http://www.postmastersart.com
Rhizome
http://rhizome.org
Runme Software Art Repository
http://www.runme.org
SFMOMA e-space
http://www.sfmoma.org/espace
SIGGRAPH Art Show
http://www.siggraph.org/artdesign
Society for Art and Technology (SAT)
http://www.sat.qc.ca
Soundtoys
http://www.soundtoys.net
STEIM
http://www.steim.org/steim
Tate Webart
http://www.tate.org.uk/netart
THE THING
http://bbs.thing.net
Turbulence
http://turbulence.org
UNESCO Knowledge Portal to the Culture section – digi-arts
http://portal.unesco.org/culture/en
V2_Organisation, Institute for the Unstable Media
http://www.v2.nl
Waag Society
http://www.waag.org
Walker Gallery 9
http://gallery9.walkerart.org
ZKM (Center for Art and Media)
http://www.zkm.de

ARTISTS' WEBSITES

Further information on the artists and artworks included in this book can be found on the websites that follow. An online list is also available on the Thames & Hudson website for this book:
http://www.thamesandhudson.com/en/1/0500238170.mxs

Abahuni, Leesa & Nicole
http://www.abahuni.org
Acevedo, Victor
http://www.acevedomedia.com
Anderson, Victor
http://www.go.to/victoranderson
Anker, Suzanne
http://www.geneculture.org
Arcangel, Cory
http://www.beigerecords.com/cory
Ashford, Rain Anne
http://www.twinkly.tv

Beasley, Bruce
http://www.brucebeasley.com
Bowen, Robert
http://www.bowenstudio.com
Briand, Mathieu
http://www.mathieubriand.com
Brown, Paul
http://www.paul-brown.com

Campbell, Jim
http://www.jimcampbell.tv
Casado, José Carlos
http://www.josecarloscasado.com
Chan, Clara
http://www-viz.tamu.edu/showcase/thswkimg
/c_chan/index.html
Collins, Dan
http://www.asu.edu/cfa/art/people/faculty/c
ollins
Collopy, Fred
http://www.rhythmiclight.com
Condon, Brody
http://www.tmpspace.com
Csuri, Charles A.
http://www.csurivision.com
Cuba, Larry
http://www.well.com/user/cuba

Davies, Char
http://www.immersence.com

Deck, Andy
http://artcontext.net
http://andyland.net
Doherty, Robin
http://www.arraystudios.co.uk
Domingues, Diana
http://artecno.ucs.br
Dove, Toni
http://www.tonidove.com

Eber, Dena Elisabeth
http://art.bgsu.edu
Em, David
http://www.davidem.com
Epuré, Sherban
http://www.serban-epure-letitzia-bucur.com

Farkas, Tamás F.
http://www.geocities.com/tamasffarkas/1.html
Fenster, Diane
http://www.dianefenster.com
Field, Michael
http://nothung.math.uh.edu/~mike
Finnegan, John Campbell
http://www.tech.purdue.edu/newalbany/facult
yandstaff/fac_finnegan.cfm
Fisher, Rob
http://robfisheramericandream.com
http://www.sculpture.org/robfisher
Fry, Benjamin
http://acg.media.mit.edu/people/fry/
valence
Fujihata, Masaki
http://www.fujihata.jp

Galloway, Alexander R.
http://itserve.cc.ed.nyu.edu/galloway
Galloway, Kit
http://www.ecafe.com
Gardiner, Jeremy
http://www.jeremygardiner.co.uk
Gartel, Laurence
http://www.gartelmuseum.com

Geib, Dona
http://www.clevelandart.org/private/tas/html/
2744775.html
Goldberg, Ken
http://www.ken.goldberg.net
Golden, Helen
http://www.helengolden.com
Gollifer, Sue
http://dam.org/gollifer

Haig, Ian
http://www.ianhaig.net
Hébert, Jean-Pierre
http://jeanpierrehebert.com
Hong, Wonhwa
http://www.koreanculture.org/09gallery/archi
ve2002poetry.htm
Huang, Shih-Chieh
http://www.nyfa.org/nyfa_artists_detail.asp?pi
d=36
Huff, Kenneth A.
http://www.itgoesboing.com

Iwai, Toshio
http://ns05.iamas.ac.jp/~iwai/iwai_main.html

Jodi
http://www.jodi.org
Johnson, Chris S.
http://www.csj2.com
Jones, Bill
http://firstpulseprojects.com/bill.html

Kac, Eduardo
http://www.ekac.org
Kawaguchi, Yoichiro
http://www.iii.u-tokyo.ac.jp/~yoichiro
Kerlow, Isaac
http://www.artof3d.com/kerlow.htm
Klima, John
http://www.glasbead.com
Knowlton, Ken
http://www.knowltonmosaics.com

IMAGE CREDITS

Images are referred to by page number.
All images are copyright the artist unless otherwise stated.

68 Robert Michael Smith, *Jogae Dentata*, 1999.
Photo: Robert Michael Smith.
68 Javier Roca, *X/Y Machina*, 2000.
69 Lillian Schwartz, *Flower 1A*, 2000.
Courtesy Lillian Feldman Schwartz Collection,
Ohio State University.
All rights reserved.
69 Sergio Spada, *Evolution*, 2000.
70 Roman Verostko, *Cyberflower IV, Gold Version*,
2000.
Courtesy of Roman Verostko.
71 Joan Truckenbrod, *Artificial Frame*, 1994.
Courtesy of FLATFILEgalleries, Chicago, IL.
72 Anna Ursyn, *Monday Morning*, 1995.
72 James Faure Walker, *F-G The Restless Inventor
of Cinema*, 2000.
73 Michael Wright, *The Light*, 1992.
73 Liu Wei, *Forbidden City Series No. 1*, 2000.
74 Mark Wilson, *PSC31*, 2003.
Photo courtesy of Mark Wilson.
75 Bruce Wands, *Buddha Light Painting #4*, 2004.

CHAPTER 3:
DIGITAL SCULPTURE
80 Bruce Beasley, *Breakout*, 1991.
Photo: Lee Fatheree.
81 (l) Bruce Beasley, *Outreach*, 1998.
Photo: Lee Fatheree.
81 (r) Bruce Beasley, *Insurgent*, 2001.
Photo: Lee Fatheree.
82 (a) Suzanne Anker, *Origins and Futures*, 2004.
Courtesy of the Suzanne Anker and Universal
Concepts Unlimited.
80 (b) Suzanne Anker, *Origins and Futures*, 2004.
Courtesy of the Suzanne Anker and Universal
Concepts Unlimited.
83 (a) Dan Collins, *Speaking Like Adults*,
1993–2003.
Photo: Robert Lopardo.
83 (b) Dan Collins, *Twister*, 2003.
84 Dan Collins, *Return to the Garden*, 2003.
Photo Credit: Gene Cooper.
86 (a) Kenneth Snelson, *Star Landing*, 1990.
Courtesy of Kenneth Snelson.
86 (b) Kenneth Snelson, *Forest Devils' Moon Night*,
1990. Courtesy of Kenneth Snelson.
87 Kenneth Snelson, *Chain Bridge Bodies*, 1991.
Courtesy of Kenneth Snelson.
88 Anna Ursyn, *Hero Horse*, 1989.
89 Peter Terezakis, *Sound Blinker*, 1983. Courtesy
of Peter Terezakis.
89 (a) James Seawright, *Orion*, 2002.
Courtesy of James Seawright and OK Harris
Gallery, New York, NY.
89 (b) James Seawright, *House Plants*, 1984,
Courtesy of James Seawright and OK Harris
Gallery, New York, NY.
90 Michael Rees, *Putto8 2x2x2x2 V2*, 2003.
91 Michael Rees, *Putto8 2x2x2x2*, 2003.
92 (l) Rob Fisher, *Protos*, 2001.
Computer graphics visualization:
J. Christopher Forman.
92 (r) Rob Fisher, *Dihedrals*, 2002. Computer
graphics visualization: Mary Vollero.
93 (a) Christian Lavigne, *L'Age du Fer*, 2002.

93 (b) Christian Lavigne, *Cybersaly 3:
Le Secret de l'Etre*, 2002–03.
94 Mark Millstein, *Frequency Kite 2*, 2003.
Copyright and photo: Mark Millstein
95 (a) David Curt Morris, *Rainmaker*, 2001.
95 (b) David Curt Morris, *Rainmaker*, 2001.
96 (l) Corinne Whitaker, *New Beginnings*, 2001.
96 (r) Corinne Whitaker, *Sculpt 1.3.00D*, 2000.
97 (a) Robert Michael Smith,
Ephesiancybergin, 2003.
Photo: Robert Michael Smith.
97 (b) Robert Michael Smith,
Gynefleuroceraptor, 2003.
Photo Robert Michael Smith.

CHAPTER 4:
DIGITAL INSTALLATION AND
VIRTUAL REALITY
102 Mathieu Briand, *SYS*05.ReE*03/SE*1
\MoE*2-4*, 2000.
Photo Credit: Bruno Amsellem.
102 Brody Condon and Shih-Chieh Huang,
DeResFX.Kill(KarmaPhysics, < 5.0Amp), 2003.
Made possible by a grant from Franklin Furnace.
103 José Carlos Casado and Harkaitz Cano,
Pandora's Box (revisited).v03, 2001.
104 Char Davies, *Seeds, Ephémère*, 1998.
105 Char Davies, *Forest Stream, Ephémère*, 1998.
106 Diane Fenster, *The Secrets of the Magdalen
Laundries* (detail), 2000.
Composer: Michael McNabb,
www.mcnabb.com
107 Masaki Fujihata, *Beyond Pages*, 1995–97.
108 Jeremy Gardiner, *Spring – Purbeck Light
Years*, 2003.
Creative direction and artwork:
Jeremy Gardiner.
Programming: Anthony Head.
Production: Veronica Falcao.
109 (a) Jeremy Gardiner, *Winter –
Purbeck Light Years*, 2003.
Creative direction and artwork:
Jeremy Gardiner.
Programming: Anthony Head.
Research: Veronica Falcao.
109 (b) Jeremy Gardiner, *Purbeck Light Years*, 2003.
Creative direction and artwork: Jeremy
Gardiner. Programming: Anthony Head.
Research: Veronica Falcao.
110 Victoria Vesna, *NANO*, 2004.
Victoria Vesna and James Gimzewski,
in collaboration with architects Sharon Johnston
and Mark Lee and a creative team of media
artists and scientists.
Photo: Victoria Vesna.
110 (a) Victoria Vesna, *NANO*, 2004.
Victoria Vesna and James Gimzewski, in
collaboration with architects Sharon Johnston
and Mark Lee and a creative team of media
artists and scientists.
Photo: Victoria Vesna.
110 (b) Victoria Vesna, *NANO*, 2004.
Victoria Vesna and James Gimzewski,
in collaboration with architects Sharon
Johnston and Mark Lee and a creative

team of media artists and scientists.
Photo: Victoria Vesna.
112 Ian Haig, *Web Devolution*, 1998.
113 Shih-Chieh Huang, *RTI-#2*, 2003.
Courtesy of Shih-Chieh Huang.
114 Edwardo Kac, *Genesis*, 1999.
Courtesy Julia Friedman Gallery.
115 Edwardo Kac, *Move 36*, 2002–04.
Courtesy Julia Friedman Gallery.
116 Grahame Weinbren, *Frames*, 1999.
Computer, laser disc players, peripheral
equipment including custom dissolve unit
designed and built by Jim Campbell.
Producer: Sandra McLean.
117 Noah Wardrip-Fruin, Sascha Becker,
Josh Carroll, Robert Coover, Andrew McClain
and Shawn Greenlee, *Screen*, 2003–05.
Image created by Josh Carroll.
Figure in image: Michelle Higa.
Courtesy of the artists.
118 (a) David Rokeby, *Giver of Names*,
1991 – present.
Photo: Robert Keziere.
118 (b) David Rokeby, *Giver of Names*,
1991 – present. Photo: David Rokeby.
119 Federico Muelas, *Dripping Sounds*, 2002.
119 Erwin Redl, *Matrix IV* (detail), 2001.
Produced by Creative Time, New York, NY.
Courtesy of Erwin Redl.
120 Erwin Redl, *Matrix II*, 2000–03.
Courtesy of Erwin Redl.

CHAPTER 5:
PERFORMANCE, MUSIC AND SOUND ART
126 David Rokeby, *Very Nervous System*, 1986–91.
Images by William Eakin, Risa Horowitz
and Liz Garlicki.
Courtesy of Aceartinc.
127 (l) Beryl Korot and Steve Reich, *Act 1:
Hindenburg* from *Three Tales*, 2002.
Three Tales conceived and developed by
Beryl Korot (video) and Steve Reich (music).
Stage direction: Nick Mangano.
Lighting Design: Matt Frey.
Conductor: Bradley Lubman.
127 (r) Beryl Korot and Steve Reich, *Act 2: Bikini* from
Three Tales, 2002.
Three Tales conceived and developed by
Beryl Korot (video) and Steve Reich (music).
Stage direction: Nick Mangano.
Lighting Design: Matt Frey.
Conductor: Bradley Lubman.
128 Ben Neill, *Mutantrumpet*, 1990.
Photo: Bill Jones.
Courtesy Sandra Gering Gallery, New York, NY.
128 Ben Neill and Bill Jones, *Automotive Tour*, 2002.
Photo: Bill Jones.
Courtesy Sandra Gering Gallery, New York, NY.
129 Carsten Nicolai, *Performance in Montreal*, 2001.
Courtesy of Galerie EIGEN + ART
Leipzig/Berlin.
129 Carsten Nicolai in collaboration with Marko
Pelijhan, *Polar*, 2000.
Courtesy of Galerie EIGEN + ART
Leipzig/Berlin; Canon artlab, Project Atol.

130 Juan Antonio Lleó, *Torre de Espejos (Tower of Mirrors)*, 2003.

131 Juan Antonio Lleó, *Midiverso*, 1994–2000.

132 John Klima, *Glasbead*, 1999.

133 (l) Joan La Barbara, Golan Levin, Zach Lieberman and Jaap Blonk, *Messa di Voce*, 2003.
Photo: Golan Levin.

133 (r) Joan La Barbara, Golan Levin, Zach Lieberman and Jaap Blonk, *Messa di Voce*, 2003.
Photo: Golan Levin.

134 (l) Leesa and Nicole Abahuni, *Capacitance*, 2003. Commissioned by the Department of Culture and Information of Sharjah, United Arab Emirates, under the direction of His Highness Sheikh Sultan bin Muhammed Al Qasimi, Ruler of Sharjah.

134 (r) Leesa and Nicole Abahuni, *Chaotic Robotic Synesthesia*, 2000.
Support from the Experimental Television Center, Oswego, NY.

135 Rain Anne Ashford, *Dustharps*, 2000.

136 Fred Collopy, *PhiSpirals*, 2004.

137 Fred Collopy, *Wood & Water*, 2004.

138 (l) Atau Tanaka and Kasper Toeplitz, *Global String*, 2000.
Produced with financial assistance from the Daniel Langlois Foundation for Art, Science and Technology.

138 (r) Atau Tanaka and Kasper Toeplitz, *Global String*, 2000.
Photo: Gerda Seebacher.
Produced with financial assistance from the Daniel Langlois Foundation for Art, Science and Technology.

139 Peter Terezakis, *L'Autre (The Other)*, 1996.
Courtesy of Peter Terezakis.

140 Stephen Vitiello, *World Trade Center Recordings: Winds After Hurricane Floyd*, 1999. Photo: Johnna MacArthur. Courtesy of The Project, New York and Los Angeles.

141 Stephen Vitiello, *Frogs in Feedback*, 2002.
Private collection, London.

CHAPTER 6:
DIGITAL ANIMATION AND VIDEO

145 Clara Chan, *Autumn Bamboo*, 2000. This piece was created with the guidance of Prof. Carol LaFayette.

146 (a) Jim Campbell, *Church on Fifth Avenue*, 2001.

146 (b) Jim Campbell, *Motion and Rest #5 (white)*, 2002.

147 Cory Arcangel, *Urbandale Still*, 2001.
Urbandale is a commission of New Radio and Performing Arts, made possible with funding from the Jerome Foundation.

148 Larry Cuba, *3/78 (Objects and Transformations)*, 1978.

149 Larry Cuba, *Two Space*, 1979.

150 Toni Dove, *Spectropia Conjures Sally* from *Spectropia*, 1999–2002.
Written, designed and directed by Toni Dove. Actress: Aleska Palladino.

151 (a) Toni Dove, *Sally's Dressing Room* from *Sally or The Bubble Burst*, 2003.
Written, designed and directed by Toni Dove. Actress: Helen Pickett.

151 (b) Toni Dove, *Sally's Bubble Dance* from *Sally or The Bubble Burst*, 2003.
Written, designed and directed by Toni Dove. Actress: Helen Pickett.

152 (l) Yoichiro Kawaguchi, *Nebular*, 2000.

152 (r) Yoichiro Kawaguchi, *Artificial Life Metropolis Cell*, 1993.

153 Yoichiro Kuwaguchi, *Topolon*, 2001.

154 Dennis H. Miller, *Faktura 2*, 2003.
Courtesy of Dennis H. Miller, Northeastern University.

155 Dennis H. Miller, *Vis a Vis*, 2002.
Courtesy of Dennis H. Miller, Northeastern University.

156 (l) Wayne Lytle, *Pipe Dream* from *Animusic*, 2001.
Courtesy of Wayne Lytle.

156 (r) Wayne Lytle, *Harmonic Voltage* from *Animusic*, 2001.
Courtesy of Wayne Lytle.

157 Wayne Lytle, *Acoustic Curves* from *Animusic*, 2001.
Courtesy of Wayne Lytle.

158 (l) Muntadas, *THIS IS NOT AN ADVERTISEMENT*, 1985.
Courtesy of Muntadas.

158 (r) Muntadas, 'SPEED' from *THIS IS NOT AN ADVERTISEMENT*, 1985.
Courtesy of Muntadas.

172 Karl Sims, *Particle Dreams*, 1988.
Courtesy of Karl Sims

160 (al) Karl Sims, *Panspermia*, 1990.
Courtesy of Karl Sims

160 (ar) Karl Sims, *Panspermia*, 1990.
Courtesy of Karl Sims

160 (bl) Karl Sims, *Panspermia*, 1990.
Courtesy of Karl Sims

161 Karl Sims, *Panspermia*, 1990.
Courtesy of Karl Sims

162 Opy Zouni, *Art and Industrial Product*, 2004.

163 (a) Opy Zouni, *Light/Shadow/Coincidences*, 1999.

163 (b) Opy Zouni, *Art and Car*, 2003.

CHAPTER 7:
SOFTWARE, DATABASE AND GAME ART

167 Lynn Hershman Leeson, *Synthia*, 2000–02, Artist: Lynn Hershman Leeson in cooperation with Lior Saar.
Fabricator: Matt Heckert.
Administrator: Michael Ahearn.
Coordinator: Kyle Stephan.
Web design and production: Sandra D. Zimmermann, Berlin.
Designers: Sean Ahlquist, Matt Whitman, Ben de Leon and Digital Core.
Additional software: Michael Greenspon, Sequin Corporation. Collection of Donald Hess.

168 Alexander R. Galloway and RSG, *CarnivorePE*, 2001.
Courtesy of Alexander R. Galloway.

169 Russet Lederman, *American Views: Stories of the Landscape*, 2001.
Commissioned by the Smithsonian American Art Museum.

169 Josh On, *They Rule*, 2001.
Artwork map created by Chris MacGregor.

170 (a) John F. Simon, Jr., *Color Panel v1.0*, 1999.
Courtesy of John F. Simon, Jr.

170 (b) John F. Simon, Jr., *ComplexCity*, 2000.
Courtesy of John F. Simon, Jr.

171 John F. Simon, Jr., *Every Icon*, 1996
Courtesy of John F. Simon, Jr.

172 Golan Levin, *Floccus*, 1999.
Courtesy of Golan Levin.

172 Golan Levin, *Yellowtail*, 1999.
Courtesy of Golan Levin.

173 Golan Levin, Scott Gibbons and Gregory Shakar, *Scribble*, 2000.
Courtesy of Golan Levin.

174 Michael Field, *Armies of the Night*, 2000.

175 George Legrady, *Pockets Full of Memories*, 2001. (Interactive installation.)
Produced in collaboration with Dr Timo Honkela, Media Lab, University of Art and Design Helsinki, (Kohonen self-organizing neural-net algorithm); C3 Center for Culture and Communication, Budapest (touchscreen data collection, hardware and software); Projekttriangle, Stuttgart, (design and visual identity); Andreas Schlegel, (visualization programming); CREATE lab, UC Santa Barbara, (web software development). With the financial assistance of the Daniel Langlois Foundation for Art, Science and Technology, Montreal; Centre Georges Pompidou, Paris; and the Office of Research, UC Santa Barbara.

176 George Legrady, *Contributed Objects, Pockets Full of Memories* (Data Visualization), 2001.
See 191.

178 Marek Walczak and Martin Wattenberg, *Apartment*, 2001.
Courtesy of Marek Walczak and Martin Wattenberg.

179 Marek Walczak and Martin Wattenberg, *Apartment*, 2001.
Courtesy of Marek Walczak and Martin Wattenberg.

180 (l) Cory Arcangel, *I Shot Andy Warhol*, 2002.
Courtesy of Team Gallery and the Beige Programming Ensemble.

180 (r) Cory Arcangel, *I Shot Andy Warhol*, 2002.
Courtesy of Team Gallery and the Beige Programming Ensemble.

180 Kathleen Ruiz, *Bang, Bang (you're not dead?)*, 2000.

181 Kathleen Ruiz, *Stunt Dummies*, 2003.

182 W. Bradford Paley, *TextArc*, 2002.
Courtesy of W. Bradford Paley.

CHAPTER 8:
NET ART

188 (l) Jodi, *Untitled Game*, 2000.
Courtesy of the %20 Artist.

188 (r) Jodi, *CTRL-SPACE*, 1998.
Courtesy of the %20 Artist.

189 Jodi, *My%Desktop*, 2003.

Courtesy of the %20 Artist.

190 (a) Ken Goldberg, *Telegarden*, 1995–2004.
Co-directors: Ken Goldberg and
Joseph Santarromana.
Project team: George Bekey, Steven Gentner,
Rosemary Morris Carl Sutter, Jeff Wiegley,
Erich Berger.
Photo: Robert Wedemeyer.

190 (b) Ken Goldberg, Randall Packer,
Gregory Kuhn and Wojciech Matusik,
Mori, 1999– present.
Concept and direction: Ken Goldberg.
Sound composition and design: Randall Packer.
Physical and acoustical design: Gregory Kuhn.
Internet and display software: Wojciech Matusik.
Thanks to Berkeley Seismographic Lab (Lind
Gee, Doug Neuhouser, Barbara Romanowicz).
Live seismic data feed: NTT InterCommunication
Center and support for Version 1.0.
Sound System: Meyer Sound Laboratories.
Software Support: CNMAT, UC Berkeley.
Builder: Pamela Beitz. Production: Zakros
InterArts. Curation: Steve Dietz.

191 (a) Lynn Hershman Leeson, *Agent Ruby's
Edream Portal*, 2002.
Courtesy of Bitforms Gallery, New York, NY
and Gallery Paule Anglim, San Francisco, CA.

191 (b) Lynn Hershman Leeson, *Agent Ruby Mood
Swing Diagram*, 2002.
Courtesy of Bitforms Gallery, New York, NY
and Gallery Paule Anglim, San Francisco, CA.

192 Victoria Vesna, *Bodies© INCorporated*,
1996 (4 views).
Produced in collaboration with Jason Schleifer,
Ken Fields and Robert Nideffer.

193 Victoria Vesna, *Bodies© INCorporated*, 1996.
Produced in collaboration with Jason Schleifer,
Ken Fields and Robert Nideffer.

194 Diana Domingues, *Serpentarium*, 2000.
Produced by Diana Domingues/ARTECHNO
Group. NTAV laboratory of Research: New
Technologies in Visual Arts, University of Caxias
do Sul/CNPq, Brazil.
Thanks to CNPq-Conselho Nacional de
Desenvolvimento Cientifico e Tecnologico;
FAPERGS-Fundacao de Amparo à Pesquisa do
Estado do Rio Grande do Sul; UCS Universidade
de Caxias do Sul.

195 Diana Domingues, *I N S N (H) A K (R) E S*,
2000–01.
Produced by Diana Domingues/ARTECHNO
Group. NTAV laboratory of Research: New
Technologies in Visual Arts, University of Caxias
do Sul/CNPq, Brazil.
Thanks to CNPq-Conselho Nacional de
Desenvolvimento Cientifico e Tecnologico;
FAPERGS-Fundacao de Amparo à Pesquisa do
Estado do Rio Grande do Sul; UCS Universidade
de Caxias do Sul.

197 Andy Deck, *Glyphiti*, 2001 – present.
Frame from 8 August 2003.
Courtesy of artcontext.net.

198 (l) Muntadas, *The File Room*, 1994.
Courtesy of Muntadas.

198 (r) Muntadas, *On Translation:
The Internet Project*, 1996.
Courtesy of Muntadas.

199 Patrick Lichty, *Sprawl*, 2000.
Courtesy of Patrick Lichty.

200 Maciej Wisniewski, *3 Seconds in the Memory
of the Internet*, 2002.
Courtesy of Postmasters Gallery, New York, NY.

201 Maciej Wisniewski, *netomat™*, 1999.
Courtesy of Postmasters Gallery, New York, NY.

201 Adrianne Wortzel, *Dream Sequence* from
Eliza Redux, 2004.
Developed at StudioBlue, the Cooper Union for
the Advancement of Science and Art, New York,
with support from a Franklin Furnace Fund for
Performance Art Grant.

202 Alexander R. Galloway, Mark Tribe and Martin
Wattenberg, *StarryNight*, 1999.

203 (a) Annette Weintraub, *Life Support (patient
room)*, 2003.

203 (b) Annette Weintraub, *Life Support (surgery)*,
2003.

204 (l) Rafael Lozano-Hemmer, *Vectorial Elevation,
Relational Architecture 4*, 1999–2004.

204 (r) Rafael Lozano-Hemmer, *Vectorial Elevation*,
Relational Architecture 4, 1999–2004.

205 Rafael Lozano-Hemmer, *Vectorial Elevation*,
Relational Architecture 4, 1999–2004.
Photo: Martin Vargas.

INDEX